PREFACE

Welcome to the *Youth Makerspace Playbook*! Our goal is to help guide and inspire you in crafting spaces that are reflections of everyone in your community, especially the youth who will be benefiting from them (throughout this book, "youth" refers to children of all ages). We hope these pages will be a catalyst for your explorations, internet searches, and further reading.

The numbers of makerspaces, and the resources supporting them, have grown tremendously in recent years, along with the stories of their impact, communities of practice, and support for maker educators. As this playbook is intended to be a complement to existing resources and the still-relevant material of the *Makerspace Playbook: School Edition*, we began our process with a needs assessment, asking educators what they found most useful in the *School Edition* and what was desired in a new playbook. Producing "Makerspaces: Highlights of Select Literature" gave us a further sense of the makerspace landscape. Results of these efforts reinforced our desire to honor the growing diversity of makerspaces in all kinds of settings, including libraries, museums, schools, and community-based organizations. We also wished to represent the entire spectrum of space types and complexity, from simple and small to large well-appointed spaces.

Although this playbook is primarily intended for those just getting started in developing youth makerspaces, we hope that even experienced spacemakers will draw inspiration from the content. After all, a hallmark of most makerspaces is that they're continually being remade. Much of our source material is drawn from an extensive site survey completed by a dedicated group of maker educators from various levels of experience (see Acknowledgements). For further information and resources, check out this playbook's web page and the Spaces & Places section of Maker Ed's Resource Library. If you're at a slightly different point in your journey and need help convincing administrators and community members of the value of creating a makerspace, you may find the Making the Case section valuable as well.

As you read this playbook, we encourage you to take notes about what excites and intrigues you. Sketch ideas for possible layouts, doodle in the margins, make lists of materials, tools, and project possibilities. Involve your young audience at every stage possible. Asking your future users to describe and draw their dream makerspaces and inquiring about their interests, experience, and curiosities are great ways of involving youth in the planning process, helping to build ownership and make the space truly theirs. Throughout the book are several invitations to record and explore everyone's ideas and inspirations. We'd love to see these shared on our social media and online community.

Maker Ed

It's an exciting time of increasingly powerful and affordable technologies, providing new possibilities for countless forms of making. It's also an opportunity to honor and learn from the historical aspects of making, such as traditional crafts, arts, humanities, artisanship, and inventions, as well as the people who helped propel our innovations to where they are today. So, while we look forward, we also look back, for inspiration, tools, approaches, and ideas, all with the intention of fulfilling our obligation to provide every child with opportunities to express themselves in countless forms of creativity, connect with each other and their community, and contribute to society. We're here to make things, and in doing so, make things better for each other. Together, let's make the space for it all to happen!

TABLE OF CONTENTS

This work was created in part by the entire Maker Ed staff, with specific contributions by Steve Davee, Goli Mohammadi, Lisa Regalla, and Stephanie Chang.

MakerEd.org | @MakerEdOrg | /MakerEducationInitiative | @MakerEdInitiative

The Maker Education Initiative is a non-profit project of the Tides Center, Tax ID: 94-321-3100

GETTING STARTED

Let's begin with memory and imagination. Think back on some of your earliest, fondest memories of making something. Was it building with blocks? Tunneling in the sand? Writing lines of code or singing your own silly songs? Drawing, painting, or telling a story?

Chances are, whatever the memory, you also recall the feelings that accompanied creation: the joy of play, the wonder of discovering some secret of a material, the simple pleasure of doodling, writing, dancing, sewing, or building. Take a moment to think about how these experiences may have had lasting influences on you and the choices you've made. These memories, in fact, helped to make you.

Now think about the environments that fostered these experiences. What was it about the settings that invited, allowed, encouraged, or even required you to make something? Who, if anyone, contributed to those environments? Peers, teachers, guardians, or perhaps siblings? Something about those environments allowed making to happen and perhaps even had an influence over what you made, how you made it, and what you thought of it. Making was, in part, made possible by the space and the people in it.

Makerspaces are such places of possibilities, bringing together people, parts, and potential. They're environments that foster not just creations but also connections, community, and memories. On the most basic level, makerspaces are any places, real or virtual, that enable acts of making.

If you're starting a makerspace, or seeking to improve or expand an existing space, our shared mission is to help shape confident, capable, compassionate, and creative citizens. Countless educators have experienced how the kinds of opportunities provided by caring, dynamic, and exciting environments, such a makerspaces, can be utterly influential and empowering.

Let's get mentally started by imagining the best spaces we can and then plan on ways to start making them happen for as many children who can benefit from them as possible. After all, if we're shaped in large part by our experiences, we owe it to every child to help create the best and most memorable experiences possible.

Maker Ed

Many Kinds of Makerspaces

Makerspaces exist in many forms, at all levels of complexity. Perhaps the most important point to stress at first is that you're free to make your space, with the consideration and collaboration of your learners, in any way you see fit. Individuality is a hallmark of the best creative spaces, and this is certainly true of makerspaces, as we show through the many examples presented in this playbook.

We'll often refer to a makerspace as a single space, but it's important to note that many makerspaces are not single, dedicated places. Making may be happening, for example, throughout entire libraries, schools, institutions, or museums.

Makerspaces can also exist in temporary forms, as well as in mobile formats. For now, we won't limit your thoughts with definitions or lists of space types. Rather, think, "What is it about any space that I have access to use that can enable making?" Is it things like building cardboard forts on the playground? Dance choreography in the cafeteria? Games on a table or cart in a general exhibit space? A table in the lobby of a library filled with construction set materials?

Whatever your space assets happen to be, whether you have a new dedicated space or a small part of an existing space, the potential of any makerspace is less about the actual physical space and more about the people and programming in it.

Start Simply

The advice to "just get started, simply" is among the most common. We'll use this chapter as a brief overview, focusing on ways to get started creating or improving makerspaces. Later chapters will cover more detailed discussions of spaces, materials, tools, and facilitation. Finally, we'll consider sustainability: keeping spaces thriving, accessible, and connected to communities.

Your Greatest Resources

Perhaps most importantly, we recommend collecting interests, hopes, and ideas from the youth who will be using the space. This will help drive the space's ability to be youth-centered.

Sample questions for youth:
o   What do you enjoy doing most when you have free time?
o   Is there anything that you'd really love to build, make, and/or invent?
o   What are the things you see yourself good at when it comes to helping others?
o   In what ways do you enjoy helping people the most?
o   What are you curious about?
o   What are some things you're most excited to learn or get better at?
o   Is there anything that makes you nervous that you'd like more practice and help with?
o   Think about your favorite space (a room in your home or school, or even a space outside). Why is it your favorite? What do you like about it?
o   If you could add anything to your favorite space, what would it be and why?

Gathering responses to these questions provides a powerful, tangible starting reference. While the answers can be incredibly inspiring, they can also be overwhelming. We recommend looking for commonalities. Once you've collected feedback from the youth, you can make an assessment of your resources and find the project intersections where those resources and the needs of the youth intersect. We've provided a form in Appendix A to help you think about what you hope to achieve, what you already have, what you absolutely need, and what you might easily obtain. This sheet will help you focus on what is possible when beginning, even without much (or any) financial support.

Getting Mentally Started

Makerspaces, like making, are all about ways of thinking. Let's get into a spacemaker frame of mind. Effective and successful spacemakers tend to:

- See possibilities in all things, especially the resources they already have
- View their community of users as their greatest resource and asset
- Include youth in the development and growth of the space and programming (You've already started by gathering feedback to the aforementioned questions!)
- Recognize, welcome, and celebrate user interests
- Encourage and make visible the ways that youth can support each other and celebrate the gifts they bring to the community
- Provide materials and tools that allow for flexibility and encourage reuse and open-ended exploration
- Foster a culture of sharing and support
- Create an environment that is welcoming, inclusive, and sensitive to the needs of all learners
- Provide a space and culture that is physically, socially, and emotionally safe

This mindset is discussed in further detail in the "Approaches & Practices" chapter. In general, hallmarks of effective spaces are those that provide multiple options, encourage cross-pollination of varied creative pursuits, and foster ways to share and learn skills within a supportive, diverse, and vibrant community.

Finding and Making Space

Let's consider some of the simplest places to make. Working surfaces such as tables, counters, or desks are often enough. Young children, especially, are inclined to use floors as working and playing surfaces. Utilizing existing space, adapting or transforming spaces used for other purposes, and creating mobile or pop-up spaces are examples we explore in "Makerspaces: Highlights of Select Literature." Many educators start by stocking a small corner table, cabinet, closet, or counter with supplies that can be brought out into larger general-use spaces, such as classrooms.

Increasingly, many makerspaces actually exist in the form of mobile carts. Such uses encourage flexibility, efficient storage, and focused materials, as well as emphasize quality of offerings over quantity and variety. This is one place to consider beginning. What would you put on your maker cart?

MakerEd

We encourage you to think flexibly and creatively about space and to look for opportunities to share space if necessary, which may even lead to serendipitous opportunities to collaborate with other users of these spaces. We'll take a deeper look at different types of makerspaces in the "Places to Make" chapter.

Material Matters

Even the most mundane of materials can become fascinating and powerful depending on their invitation of use. Paper is a well-known example—ubiquitous, versatile, and either taken for granted or incredibly creatively empowering, depending on how its use is invited. Arts and crafts materials, as well as other office supplies, are further simple staples.

The most efficient materials are those that can be reused. Construction sets, hardware, and salvaged components all can be used and reused in a large variety of projects and explorations. Also effective are materials that can be readily obtained from recycling channels, such as cardboard (a clear favorite of many a makerspace) and used plastic containers. Makerspaces commonly make extensive use of materials that may otherwise end up in the landfill, providing another use cycle for these materials.

Nature also provides some of the best sources for making. Sticks, leaves, mud, clay, sand, and rocks are all primordial materials that likely have figured in many happy making memories. Natural materials are versatile, beautiful, abundant, and of course environmentally beneficial when responsibly gathered.

Even the simplest of makerspaces must still contend with storage issues, so think early on about where and how you might store items in progress and materials for use. We discuss materials in further detail and share specific examples of storage and organizational systems in the "Materials & Tools" chapter.

Tool Talk

When considering creating a makerspace, perhaps one of the biggest areas of inhibition (and excitement) is tools. We're here to help you get past some common perceptions that often hinder makerspace initiation and development. There are no required or special tools needed to "qualify" a space as a makerspace. We're looking at you, 3D printers; we know you can be awesome, but a makerspace you do not define.

Look instead to the varieties of making that you hope to support. What can you do with what you already have, such as scissors or the ubiquitous glue gun? How about some screwdrivers? Paint brushes? An old laptop, out-of-date cellphone, or tablet?

Even older computers can often handle many of the free programs that allow a myriad of making options, including coding, graphic design, music editing, and even video and animation creation. Replenishing an older machine with a simple operating system like Linux works great. There are increasingly affordable and powerful ways to connect analog offerings with digital tools.

Your equipment inventory can be one that grows over time. When you're just getting started, the focus is on using what you already have most effectively, through the projects, programming, and options your space invites and supports. Organic collections of tools may even innately reflect the interests of the people and projects in your space; for example, you may start out with more woodworking tools than coding tools, and that's perfectly fine.

Finally, no matter what is said about tools, equipment, space, and materials, the real center of any space is the people and their possibilities. Children show us constantly, through play, what they can make with the absolute minimum of materials and space, often with no tools at all. As adults, we can leverage the power of play and curiosity to provide experiences that honor this foundation and are augmented, rather than limited, by the physical stuff. In short, you can do a heck of a lot with very little in the way of materials and tools, as we explore further in the "Materials & Tools" chapter.

Beginning with Play and Imagination

Let's consider some starting points, beginning with the areas of youth expertise we've mentioned: play and imagination. Outlets of artistic expression are extremely important for makerspaces. Besides providing basic art and craft materials, you may consider inviting the creation of stories and encouraging their capture and expression through writing, skits and plays, videos, animation, or songs, to name a few options. This can serve to invigorate ideas in any subject area. A story can be shown and told in many ways. There's a reason storytelling is among the oldest and most fundamental forms of making.

Tinkering approaches make use of playful inclinations and curiosity. Commonly, tinkering is all about seeing the possibilities of materials through open-ended exploration. Projects may emerge from simply messing around with materials. It's a state of play that has tremendous value, even if it doesn't lead to a particular project or product. In tinkering, it's fundamentally about the process, and it's an easy way to start.

One common tinkering mantra is to "start by taking apart." Providing interesting things to disassemble, such as obsolete electronics and e-waste, is a foundational way to invite anyone into a making experience. Disassembly can also serve as a low-stress way to learn how to use tools. Using the found, salvaged, or harvested materials—whether in a collage, parts for a robot, or sources of construction materials for any number of projects—then provides an origin story about where the parts came from that adds character and meaning. To help keep things safe and efficient, we've provided tips and safety guidelines for gathering and disassembling e-waste in Appendix B.

Tinkering approaches are among many mindsets and facilitation methods we'll discuss in further detail in the "Approaches & Practices" chapter. No matter what your current educational experience and background, there are many inspirational, effective philosophies and methods to learn from and blend.

Your Greatest Collaborators

For all that can be daunting about makerspace development, you have no need to be alone in the process, considering your audience. Youth are your greatest assets and collaborators. Makerspaces are places where powerful capabilities in everyone, at every age, can be discovered, shared, and nurtured, to the benefit of the entire community. Imagine the ways in which you might honor emerging skills and interests by inviting opportunities for youth to share, teach, mentor, and take ownership over essential responsibilities. Think of the joy and empowerment such recognition and trust engenders.

Spaces can make what's important to youth visible and valued in ways that are likewise transformative and empowering. They can spark new interests and deepen existing enthusiasm. When a space clearly communicates that personal interests are encouraged, connected, and created, you'll be invigorated by the community that arises. A shared sense develops, that of "here's what I'm most interested in, and I'm excited for and inspired by what interests you." You'll find your own creative interests compounded by this common makerspace cultural vibe of shared excitement and appreciation. And you'll never be short of ideas and inspiration.

This shared sense of agency and ownership goes a long way toward making your space sustainable, keeping it welcoming, vibrant, and diverse in audiences and support. In the "Sustainability" chapter, we'll further explore the roles people and partnerships play in keeping spaces not just going, but thriving.

If you make the collection of ideas, dreams, abilities, and interests of your audience an integral aspect of your space from the beginning, you will have built the most important thing of all: a community of youth and adults who are agents of change and creation.

It really is all about creating possibilities and experiences that help shape attitudes, habits, and personalities in ways that are positively reinforcing. The fantastic thing is that there are countless ways to create such a culture and provide a space that is unique to your vision, participants, and community.

What's special about makerspaces is that they tend to deliberately provide a wide range of making forms and opportunities. Each range is unique and ideally co-created by all within the space.

What will be unique about your space? What surprises will you offer and what familiar staples? Once started, how will it be sustained and supported by all? How might it grow? What can it become that you cannot yet imagine? We'll keep these lofty questions in mind as we dive deeper into the details of spaces and the planning necessary to provide and enrich the best possible making experiences. ≡

PLACES TO MAKE

In this chapter, we focus on the practicalities of physical space, starting with suggestions for finding new spaces, as well as utilizing existing spaces for making. Relying on the power of examples to convey possibilities, we share several stories of makerspaces in schools, libraries, museums, and community organizations.

We also examine wider settings where children learn, play, explore, collaborate, and create to provide further inspiration and insight. Finally, we look at the environment of the makerspace, as well as logistical, social, ergonomic, and safety considerations. Whether you have it, can adapt it, or have yet to find it, your space is out there.

Seeking Spaces

Think of how many places await discovery and transformation. The possibilities of places and what they might become is exciting, and finding them can be a bit of a treasure hunt. Are there spaces being underutilized in your school, library, or museum? Even if it's only a closet, space exists that can, at the very least, serve as materials and project storage or just house a cart to be brought into common-use spaces. Though it can be daunting, seeking and finding potential in places is worth the effort. Fortunately, if you're seeking a dedicated space and starting from scratch, you're in good company. As the numbers and varieties of makerspaces continue to grow, so do examples of successes in finding space and ideas for where to begin.

The Washington Maker Workshop in San Jose, Calif., was founded by a middle school teacher, with free use of a local church's unused 100-year-old garage and adjacent land. For additional indoor space, he partnered with a fellow maker and designed and built a 224-square-foot shed, and they've shared their instructions online.

Detroit's Mt. Elliott Makerspace was likewise established in a church basement, providing a much-needed youth resource that complements the church's community-support efforts.

Baltimore's non-profit Digital Harbor Foundation founder located an empty Parks and Recreation building and turned it into the city's first free, public neighborhood makerspace.

Many communities have storefronts that have been vacant for some time. One short-term possibility is finding retail space that is in between tenants. Often, owners are willing to rent for short terms, perfect for pop-up makerspaces that can gauge community interest and prototype space. In 2013, a group of Portland, Ore., educators transformed a community center located in a former grocery store into a pop-up makerspace as a proof of concept for bringing more making opportunities to a neighborhood of high need.

Even schools sometimes have a room or closet that is not being maximized. The founder of the DIY Girls afterschool program wanted to serve the girls in the neighborhood where she grew up. She took a chance and asked the administrators at the elementary school she attended if they had any unused rooms and was thrilled to find out that her very own 5th-grade classroom was vacant. The school was happy to provide her with use of the room for the program.

Many well-established makerspaces started with very little space. For example, Toronto's aspirational 6,000-square-foot STEAMLabs makerspace for kids was started five years ago in a garage. In Miami, the REM Learning Center's Play Make Share makerspace was originally built in an old classroom, and the adjacent Fab Lab is a repurposed storage room.

Go Mini and Mobile

Photo:
Lighthouse Community
Charter School

As we mentioned in "Getting Started," makerspaces are frequently supported or created through the use of carts. This is a great way to start small and also to distribute making throughout an institution. Carts and stations on wheels can play an important role in supporting any classroom, for every subject area, with tools and materials.

In Oakland, Calif., Lighthouse Community Charter School seventh and eighth graders designed and built several mobile mini makerspaces for kindergarten classroom use. They also use carts to support outdoor making opportunities, as well as to spread the joy of making at expos and events. Likewise, Trent Miller, Library Program Coordinator for Wisconsin's Madison Public Library makerspace the Bubbler, shares, "In our media lab, we have twenty portable, up-and-working animation stations with iPads to take to youth programs around Madison."

At the Monroe Carell Jr. Children's Hospitals in Nashville, Tenn., Project M@CH (Makerspace at Children's Hospital) has assembled carts, complete with making tools and materials, to bring mini makerspaces directly to patients.

Hit the Road

Stanford University's SparkTruck has brought fun hands-on learning all across the USA since 2012. Photo: Sparktruck, used under Creative Commons 2.0 license

In the past few years, the number of makerspaces housed in vehicles, such as buses and trucks, has increased as educators seize opportunities to bring hands-on making to any location they can drive to, rather than relying on kids to be able to come to a stationary, dedicated space. Some mobile makerspaces serve as the outreach arm of a dedicated space, while others are strictly mobile with no associated brick-and-mortar location.

One strictly mobile example is San Antonio, Texas-based Geekbus, which is operated by SASTEMIC, a nonprofit STEM education-advocacy organization. Director of STEM Programs Mark Barnett recalls: "We started out as a summer makerspace located in an art museum and provided twelve weeks of Maker Camp. Once the summer was over, we started looking for a new place and stumbled upon an opportunity to go mobile. We were very fortunate to have received a bus from our sponsors Geekdom and Rackspace Hosting. We spruced up the bus with the tools and equipment from the makerspace and hit the road!"

Though it gives them opportunities to visit many schools, including surrounding rural disadvantaged communities, they are naturally restricted by space. Because the Geekbus can only hold fifteen to eighteen people at a time, they also use space outside of the bus or request space at the host location. When they come to schools, they request to use the library to set up equipment.

Roseville, Calif.-based ReCreate has two vehicles that focus on making art from reused materials. They visit 15,000 students at schools alone annually. They also run the ReCreate Art Center and Reuse Warehouse, where they offer classes and where folks can pick up supplies, paying what they can. ReCreate is currently fundraising for a third, STEAM-specific vehicle focusing on technology.

Every School a Makerspace

Besides being supported by carts, classrooms can be augmented to become versatile, self-contained makerspaces by taking on elements of larger, dedicated makerspaces. Even traditional single desks can support additional forms of making in the classroom. Many simple hand tools (drills, saws, glue guns) can be safely used directly within a classroom. With the inclusion of small, dedicated stations, possibilities further increase. Dedicated school makerspaces often support making opportunities throughout the institution, serving as a material and tool hub as well as a project and curriculum development space.

The mobile mini makerspaces we mentioned earlier at Lighthouse are part of a school-wide distribution of making. As Creativity Lab Director Aaron Vanderwerff explains, "Our program has a central, physical space—the Creativity Lab—but making is integrated into the core classrooms, and several classrooms have mini makerspaces. Making occurs in all classrooms, whether it be programming, arts and crafts, or woodworking, depending on the subject."

Similarly, many schools feature materials and tools throughout every classroom as part of ongoing projects and explorations. Opal School of the Portland Children's Museum has a combination of small dedicated studios and materials supporting inquiry-based project work in every classroom, blending every subject area. Non-profit independent school Brightworks in San Francisco is essentially a large one-room schoolroom as a makerspace, with the entire space supporting "arcs" of hands-on experiential learning through periods of exploration, expression, and exhibition.

Maker Ed

Many schools have creatively distributed making in various spaces throughout their facilities. Monticello High School, part of Albemarle County Public Schools in Charlottesville, Va., added tools and equipment, such as 3D printers, to their school library, in addition to a "genius bar," where students assist their peers with computer and digital device support. The school also converted a former storage space into a music and sound recording studio, converting and equipping it for a total of $5,000. According to the school's site, "Students and teachers alike use the space daily for everything from recording vocals, to live instrumentation, to explaining algebraic equations and wave theory." Monticello's flexibility about space and their desire to support student interests even led to a student initiating a dance troupe using the cafeteria as a makeshift dance studio.

Photo: Albemarle High School

School makerspaces often revive or take the place of traditional shops, with the new twist of being spaces that serve wider school and community populations rather than only those choosing to take shop classes. These modern shops serve not only vocational training and pathways toward further career and technical education, but they also provide valuable hand-on experiences reaching all areas of academics and student interests. In many makerspaces, traditional shop, home economics, computer, and music classes are being combined and re-envisioned for everyone.

Math teacher Casey Shea discovered an old wood and metal shop buried in a storage room at Analy High School in Sebastopol, Calif. He requested to convert it into a makerspace. Together, he and his students cleaned it up, designed the space, and built the furniture and storage systems from scratch, utilizing many of the recovered, forgotten shop tools and equipment. Besides academically supporting a wide population of students and teachers, the space aims to serve as an entrepreneurial incubator.

Castlemont High School
Fab Lab's hydroponics garden.
Photo: Maker Ed

Teachers at Castlemont High School in Oakland, Calif., transformed a former ROTC facility into a Fab Lab makerspace, even turning a former gun range into a hydroponic garden laboratory. Projects supported in the space range through STEM, arts, civics, and language subject areas. The program was developed in conjunction with Oakland's Laney College, in part to provide a career and technical pathway, bridged by similar Fab Lab spaces at the community college level.

When looking to establish spaces in any school, look to where making in many forms is already happening, such as the theater, music room, art studio, computer lab, library, and school garden. Makerspaces can augment and combine these existing forms of making, bringing together entire student populations in celebration of creativity and learning.

Every Library a Makerspace

An exciting trend for libraries is the expansion of opportunities to create, which makes sense given libraries' traditional missions of meeting community educational, cultural, recreational, social, and intellectual needs. Most libraries have historically supported many forms of making, whether it be a craft circle, scrapbook night, knitting or quilting club, computer support groups, writing workshops, or skill classes of various types. In addition, libraries have provided free access to technologies as they have emerged—think photocopy machines, printers, and the internet. It should then come as no surprise that the number of libraries expanding making opportunities and/or developing dedicated makerspaces is growing rapidly.

One example is the Maker Jawn Initiative at the Free Library of Philadelphia. (The term "jawn" is a context-dependent substitute noun that originated in the Philly hip-hop scene.)

Maker Jawn Initiative at the Free Library of Philadelphia

Project Coordinator Sarah Winchowky

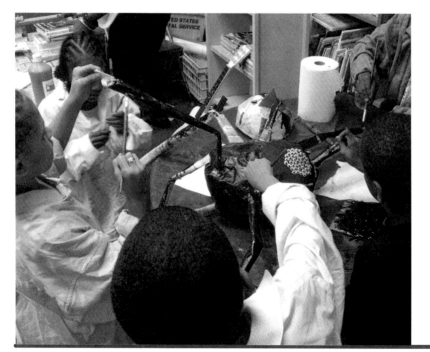

"Our programming happens across five different neighborhood libraries in Philadelphia. The space in each library is different. In some libraries, our materials share space with library books on the shelves, and programming happens directly on the library floor. In others, programming occurs in a separate room of the library.

At Kensington library, makers have a designated space that is all theirs. They use it to work, store supplies, and display their work. At Widener library, makers also have a designated room but share it with other library programs and meetings. The librarians there have given us access to a closet, where we store all our materials and supplies that we pull out for each programming session. That library also has a fenced-in, little-used parking lot with a grass section, where we go to garden and work on messier projects when it's warm out.

At Rodriguez library, the programming happens at a couple of tables located directly in the children's section of the library. At Marrero library, programming takes place in the same room as the public computer lab. This library also has a fenced-in outdoor space, where participants can sometimes go for activities such as plein air sketching.

Our intergenerational programming tends to take place on the library floor as well. Mentors will set up shop at a table, sometimes with something engaging, like the 3D printer, going to draw in potential participants. Once participants are involved and working on projects, they can do so in whatever library space makes most sense for what they're working on. In this sense, our programming is very flexible space-wise and changes to fit the needs of library staff, mentors, and participants."

Photo:
Free Library of Philadelphia

At New York's Fayetteville Free Library, housed in part in an old furniture factory, there are three different spaces to make: a Fab Lab (or as they refer to it—a Fabulous Lab) with tools ranging from sewing machines to laser cutters, a Creation Lab focused on digital media creation, and a Little Makers free play area for children ages five to eight. Community members can work on personal projects in the space after completion of certification for the use of certain tools and equipment. Fayetteville's FAQ is filled with great information on staffing, budget, promotion, and even includes a virtual tour of their space.

Gaining inspiration from tool-lending libraries, some public libraries are working to create tool and material lending programs to continue experiences for both adults and youth beyond the walls of the library. One example is the Millvale Community Library in Pittsburgh, Penn., also featured in this Maker Ed case study.

President and founder Brian Wolovich shares, "I look forward to somebody being able to walk in and check out a DVD, maybe a children's book for their kids, and a circular saw. That to me is success—people utilizing, sharing, connecting through the barter board system. Having our lending library established, set up, and organized would certainly be an outcome that I'm looking for."

At the state level, several library systems are also working to train and support librarians to create and sustain makerspaces. The Idaho Commission for Libraries has been running a program since 2012 called "Make It at the Library." As of 2015, the program provides materials, training, technical assistance, and evaluation tools to nineteen public and two school libraries throughout the state of Idaho in an effort to support collaborative efforts to reach teen and tween audiences.

For both youth and adults, these libraries serve as incubators for new thoughts and ideas, education exchange centers, and hubs for community creations and collaborations. And, as a bonus, these initiatives attract audiences to books and traditional library resources as well.

Photo: Millvale Community Library

Every Museum a Makerspace

Although museums originated as places to preserve the past, the museums of today (whether they be focused on art, history, science, or living collections such as zoos or aquariums) represent a diverse set of institutions for play and imagination to flourish. At their core is a commitment to education and public service. Many exercise this in a variety of ways, from internal programs and spaces for visitors to more outward-facing initiatives involving research, professional development, and community-based programming. Thus, many museums serve as regional hubs, supporting and inspiring making throughout their local region and beyond.

At the Children's Museum of Pittsburgh, there is a dedicated makerspace called the Makeshop, but Director of Learning and Research Lisa Brahms adds: "Makeshop is where 'making' happens in our museum, although visitors' investigation of and expression with creative processes happens throughout the entire museum! From the Studio, where visitors engage in fine art processes and concepts; to Waterplay, where visitors test and manipulate water in all forms; to the Nursery, where young learners interrogate the materials and phenomena of light, sand, and movement; to the contemporary artworks throughout the museum, making, broadly considered, happens everywhere." The Makeshop has also been a leader in research around making and learning and, after the popularity of their free annual Maker Educator Boot Camp for teachers, has expanded their professional development offerings to local and regional schools and youth-serving organizations in the area.

Photo:
Children's Museum
of Pittsburgh

Although known as a history museum, The Henry Ford in Dearborn, Mich., embodies a philosophy of "learning by doing" throughout all five of its spaces. Home to Maker Faire Detroit since 2010, programming such as their "Tinker. Hack. Invent. Saturdays" are a celebration of ingenuity for the community.

The Newark Museum in New Jersey is an institution of art, science, technology, and history. Their Makerspace at the Newark Museum connects the physical and virtual world and is part of a museum-wide effort to seamlessly blend science and art. They have even developed a partnership with Big Picture Learning in the Newark public school system to support making projects for high school students.

San Francisco's Exploratorium and its Tinkering Studio have long included making and tinkering opportunities for visitors, professional development for educators, and research into learning. Beyond their extensive in-person trainings, their free online class on the Fundamentals of Tinkering through Coursera has opened access to millions around the world interested in developing their practice around making and tinkering.

Photo:
New York Hall of Science

The Association of Science-Technology Centers (ASTC) also runs an active Community of Practice on Making & Tinkering Spaces in Museums. Many have found that a partnership with a museum (either physically or virtually) has helped advance their thinking. As you grapple with the creation of your space, don't be afraid to reach out.

Maker Ed

Every Place a Makerspace

Wherever children are given the time and space, they make things. Playing and making are children's natural modes of expression and learning, from stories co-created in dramatic play to fairy houses made in the grass. Whether it's building with blocks, making sandcastles, drawing, painting, or using chalk on the sidewalk, children have the natural capacity to take advantage of any space's support of making. They'll push the boundaries by using things in their environment in new ways, discovering hidden features and materials, and taking advantage of whatever they can get their hands on to make something. Given freedom and opportunity, the world is their makerspace. Let's consider some examples of environments that inspire creativity.

PLAYGROUNDS

Playgrounds are ideally places where society honors the importance of play. The best playgrounds provide many entry points for play, for a wide variety of ages and interests, while still providing challenge and adventure. They may include wide-open spaces to run in (e.g., athletic fields), enclosed spaces that act as forts and afford privacy, structures that challenge physically (e.g., monkey bars, swings, and merry-go-rounds), and features that inspire dramatic play.

What features and areas of your space will invite and support many forms of play, risk-taking, and inventiveness? What will be just plain fun?

Playful features to consider including in makerspaces:
- Chairs that invite movement and balance, such as rocking chairs and exercise balls
- Playfields for robot creations (such as reused FIRST Lego League playfields), micro sumo rings, or mazes and racetracks (such as Nerdy Derby tracks)
- Built-in or easily assembled ramps for wheeled and sliding creations
- Wind tubes to explore the effects of wind on various objects
- Open area for larger-scale material exploration, such as cardboard fort building or arcade-style games inspired by Caine's Arcade and Imagination Foundation's Global Cardboard Challenge

Playgrounds can be expanded in their capacity to enable making through the addition of fort-building materials. Adventure Playground in Berkeley, Calif., is a "unique outdoor facility where staff encourages children to play and build creatively" and "climb on the many unusual kid-designed and built forts, boats, and towers." In this environment, inspired by European adventure playgrounds, youth are encouraged to hammer, saw, paint, and actively work together to keep the space safe while playing and contributing to the building of an ever-changing environment.

A public Global Cardboard Challenge, planned and hosted by Opal School elementary students. Photo: Maker Ed

THEATER SPACES

Part of the beauty of theater is that it's a temporal form of art where no two shows are exactly the same. It's also an inherently social form of art that involves public gatherings to experience the performance, as well as a collection of people with varied skill sets who come together to make the show a reality.

The preparation aspect for a live performance can include a huge diversity of creative efforts and making in many forms: the writing of a play, composition and performance of music, construction of sets and props, creation of costumes, theatrical makeup, lighting, and even posters and promotion. How might these empowering aspects of theaters and studios be brought into a makerspace?
- Dramatic play area with materials to create and modify scenery, costumes, and props (even a bin of hats, sunglasses, and clothes)
- Puppet stage and screens for shadow puppets
- Musical instruments for score creation
- Clip lamps with color-changing LED bulbs controlled by phones, tablets, and computers via Bluetooth or wi-fi (These bulbs are increasingly affordable, and some even include Bluetooth speakers, enabling sound effect possibilities.)

PRODUCTION STUDIOS

Video and radio (or podcast) production studios also provide an opportunity for the more permanent capture of theatrical arts. Although the opportunities to create overlap with those of theatrical production (sets, props, lighting, etc.), there are some unique aspects that involve storyboarding, editing, and sound mixing.

At Sierra Leone's Global Minimum, youth are engaged in creating films that have deep and lasting impacts on their community. As cofounder David Sengeh shares, "In our filmmaking workshop, a group of students made a short documentary film on Kroo Bay, one of the most impoverished neighborhoods in Freetown, to portray the living conditions of people in the community. They used iMovie on iPads to edit the film, which were generously donated by Kiddify. During the Ebola crisis, students from this group created an Ebola sensitization film using the skills they learned in the filmmaking workshops."

Within the Children's Museum of Pittsburgh, there is a youth-driven radio studio, Saturday Light Brigade, which gives children's voices active community roles. By interviewing elders in each neighborhood and editing and producing a wide variety of broadcast radio shows and podcasts, young people of all ages use forms of making that bring neighborhoods and age groups together.

How might you empower these forms of expression in your makerspace?
- Stop-motion animation station (Here's a guide for classrooms and tips.)
- Green screen wall for video special effects
- Video projectors or large monitors to share media creations and inspirational videos
- Stations for recording and editing video and sound

Makerspaces can additionally serve school and community media and theater productions. We encourage you to reach out and see what is possible when combining resources, ideas, and needs.

Maker Ed

NATURE

Think of the fundamentals of playing and creating in nature: mud, sticks, leaves, rocks, and water. Natural materials help illustrate that having many of anything is interesting. Many sticks become a fort. Many grains of sand or lots of mud become structures and mud pies. Many leaves become piles to jump into. What are some simple, freely accessible things in nature you might provide in abundance in your makerspace?

Photo:
Opal School of the Portland
Children's Musuem

Nature-inspired makerspace possibilities include:

o   Water features, like water tables, to explore the material qualities of water, as well as to inspire the engineering and crafting of floating and underwater projects (Check out Riveropolis or one of many DIY options.)
o   Plants for providing decor and ambiance, as well as serving as catalysts for projects like automatic plant-watering robots and time-lapse growth videos
o   Nature bots and other tinkering creations using natural materials
o   Large amounts of simple natural materials—like leaves, stones, and sticks—for Andy Goldsworthy-inspired artistic creations
o   Miniature or tabletop sandboxes including sticks, stones, and leaves for tactile exploration and building
o   Hydroponics projects, such as this example (with tips and instructions) resulting from a partnership between Bergen County Technical School and Bergen Makerspace in Hackensack, N.J.

How might you include natural elements in your space? What might be the mud of your makerspace, gloriously messy and endlessly transformative? In the "Materials & Tools" chapter, we'll provide further examples of materials that help bring elements of nature indoors and inspire making outdoors.

ART STUDIOS AND ATELIERS

Art studios in general are environments that have traditionally invited, supported, and inspired creativity. A particular form of art studio, known as an atelier (meaning workshop in French) has been utilized by Reggio Emilia early childhood schools and Reggio-inspired educators for well over forty years. In these approaches, ateliers extend and support every aspect of learning, including social, artistic, literacy, and science. Sounds like the intention of makerspaces, doesn't it?

Ateliers are intended to provide enriching sensory experiences—often making use of light, shadow, and color—and offer ample opportunities to explore new materials and techniques, incubating new forms of expression. While the arts are the primary medium, construction, deconstruction, building, and making in countless forms are all means of exploring big ideas and questions.

Elements of studios and ateliers that can inform makerspace design and intention include:

o Abundant storage and shelving with materials highly visible, curated, and beautifully displayed
o Freely accessible materials, often sorted by type
o Ways of inviting expression and exploration through "provocations" (anything that intentionally captures attention and encourages response, such as meaningful questions, intriguing materials, or images)
o High visibility of student processes and work
o Easels, paper, and paint readily accessible
o Intriguing displays of new materials and tools that invite exploration

The look of ateliers and mini ateliers is quite unique. For inspiration, we suggest Googling images using the search term "Reggio atelier."

Ateliers set up for clay, natural material, and paint explorations. Photos: Opal School

Environment as Teacher

Makerspaces have even more to gain from the concepts behind ateliers: that of seeing the environment as the "third teacher." The other two teachers are adults and peers, whose roles we'll explore further in the chapter on "Approaches & Practices."

How and what will your environment communicate? What will it teach and show of your approaches and intentions? How will it inspire creativity and collaboration? What will it invite and what possibilities will it foster? Let's consider some important aspects of how your physical spaces educate and enable making.

SETTING THE TONE

What are the first impressions that you hope your space makes? What is welcoming about your environment? What shows youth ownership and investment? What does the space communicate? Taking the analogy of makerspace as teacher further, what is the personality of the space?

Maker Ed

As an exercise to help you think and plan for these questions, consider words and phrases that complete the following:

Ideally, when participants first enter the makerspace, they see _____.
They hear _____. They feel _____. They experience _____.
They are invited to share_____. They gain_____. They may be intrigued by_____. They may wonder about _____.

Possibilities for the blanks above might include:
o   A connection to their interests
o   A sense of community and an invitation to join it
o   Support to make things, play, explore, and discover
o   Many things that are possible
o   Familiar materials and tools
o   New, interesting, and intriguing tools and materials
o   Inspiration and ideas
o   Reasons and desire to return
o   Invitations to explore and continue
o   Questions, problems, and challenges
o   Fun and whimsy
o   Connections to academic subject areas
o   Collaboration
o   Easy ways to get started
o   That youth, their ideas and abilities, are valued
o   Ideas to take home

At the DIY Girls after-school program, the organizers focus on creating a space that is welcoming and playful with posters displaying DIY Girls expectations, journal tips, and junior mentor guidelines. They also openly display project materials, make sure to greet students as they enter, play music, and provide snacks.

Another example is the environment created on the Geekbus, which reflects their technology-focused programming. Mark Barnett of Geekbus shares, "When participants first enter the Geekbus, they see flashing colorful lights emanating from within. They hear the sound of electronic music vibrating from the subwoofers. They feel excited to go in and see what's going on. They experience a presentation and hands-on learning experience about robotics, computer programming, or 3D printing. They leave with wonder, inspiration, and a desire to learn more."

There are many practical ways these messages can be communicated: through the use of signage, documentation, display of projects, and tools and materials availability. Open display of projects and prototypes that might not have worked, as well as projects in all stages of completion, shows a respect for process and transparency. It's also important to ask not just what is on your wall but who. Do the walls reflect the community and inclusion for all demographics? Do those who enter see examples of themselves reflected in the space?

We'll revisit the idea of tone, as well as explore ways of building community and culture into the space, in the "Sustainability" chapter. What will be the tone—or rather the multiple tones—that become the music of your space?

OPEN SPACE

Wide-open areas and abundant table space are among the ideals of providing for possibilities and communicating a sense of comfort and breathing room, especially when collaboration is involved. Bear in mind that "open" doesn't necessarily mean "big"; a small space can still be open. At Toronto's STEAMLabs, Andy Forest shares, "The great hall is the majority of the space. This is filled with workbenches and lined with tools and materials. We believe that a big part of innovation is bumping in to other interesting people and projects. The cross collaboration that happens in an ad-hoc manner is facilitated by having as many people in close proximity to each other as possible. With this in mind, we have as big an open area as possible. Ceiling noise dampening panels control the sound from being too loud."

Cluttered and cramped areas can quickly become physically and psychologically stifling. Clutter is a constant battle. To help control it, think of including or adapting an area where clutter can be quickly hidden, or at least managed behind the scenes, to help keep spaces open. Storage bins under tables or a well-managed closet can help.

While it's ideal for tools and materials to be visible and accessible, not everything has to be out at once; a few of something being visible could represent many available in storage. And while wide-open spaces can open possibilities for some young makers, smaller, cozier spaces can also provide a sense of comfort for others. This balance of clutter versus cleanliness is one of the most individual aspects of spaces. We hope you find your own balance and comfort in knowing it's a juggling act for all.

An open space also means that it's open and accessible for everyone in the community, regardless of their age, ability, or status. Creating such a space isn't just a nice thing to do—it's the right thing. Washington University offers excellent guidelines for makerspace accessibility and universal design, and the Center for Applied Special Technology (CAST) has a variety of resources for learning environments. Organizations such as DIY Ability provide outstanding examples for DIY approaches to enable communication, mobility, and self-expression. By being thoughtful about universal design, a makerspace can transform into a more inclusive, welcoming, and safe environment for learning.

AREAS TO SOCIALIZE, THINK, AND RELAX

Be sure to provide space for youth to gather, plan, communicate, and share ideas. You might offer whiteboards or even cover entire table surfaces in whiteboard material (shower board material is a cost-effective alternative), paper, or blackboard paint. At the Chicago Public Library's Maker Lab, the walls are made of whiteboard material, to allow brainstorming to happen all around. Accessibility to simple materials, such as paper and craft materials, construction sets, and interesting small objects can also help with conceptual incubation. It's often useful to think with objects, so having items that invite play and prototyping, such as construction sets (discussed in detail in the "Materials & Tools" chapter), promotes planning and brainstorming.

Maker Ed

Couches provide popular social space for sharing music-making ideas at A3 House. Photo: Albemarle High School

The Children's Museum of Pittsburgh's Makeshop has a cozy corner by the window, with comfortable chairs, a rug, and a bookshelf stocked with a wide variety of books that inspire and support the many forms of making in the space. The inclusion of this area communicates that there is a space to take a break, enjoy a book, sit, relax, and even just look out the window. Areas like this are important to include for those who may be overwhelmed at times by the sheer amount of stuff and possibilities of makerspaces.

Many makerspaces include a lounge-type area that allows for breaks, supports social interactions and discussion, and provides inspiring reading material. It's amazing how much a couch, a hammock, or even a single comfy chair can communicate about a space's friendliness and warmth. Many ideas and collaborations are born out of casually hanging out. Building in features that invite social connections will go a long way toward fostering peer-to-peer support and inspiration.

HEIGHT PERSPECTIVES

When a child enters a space, especially for the first time, they perceive things differently than adults in many ways, and this can vary greatly depending on their age and height. The height perspective of wheelchair users is likewise important. Taking these considerations into account makes a big difference in making what should be visible more so and obscuring what is aesthetically undesired.

Here's a simple guideline to help gain a child's perspective: take a look throughout your environment while kneeling. For most adults, this brings you nearer to the heights of the average eight to ten-year-old. Sitting on the floor approximates the heights of toddlers near two years old.

Photo: Opal School

What differences do you see in your environment from these perspectives? What becomes less visible or hidden, and what becomes more visible or revealed? You may also see things obscured that should be immediately visible, such as safety gear, first aid supplies, and any warning signs.

ROLES OF LIGHT

Abundant, natural light is ideal, when you can get it. When relying on artificial light, getting creative with multiple sources of light can help distinguish areas by color and light level. The use of light tables as construction surfaces is particularly photogenic and helps provide inviting and attractive lighting ambience. Use of dark spaces can be inspiring for encouraging explorations with light. A playful approach to inviting light explorations is to use old overhead projectors (lots of these are still around, often unused), where shadows and colors projected on the walls can be tinkered with depending on what happens on the overhead projector's bed.

Tinkering with ultraviolet light, LEDs, water, dish soap, and dry ice. Photo: CoLab Tinkering

Overall, given the choice between LED and fluorescent sources, LEDs are worth the moderate extra expense. Many children are acutely aware of and distracted by the flickering, poor light quality of fluorescent lighting. Light is so important in setting mood, supporting work, and providing comfort. It's much more than a mere utility—it's something to tinker and make with. What light will you bring into your space?

Utility Considerations

Though utility logistics aren't always the most fun to entertain, they're important for creating a space that is functional, safe, and practical.

RECYCLING, REFUSE, AND SCRAP BINS

Don't forget to provide space and means for accommodating recycling and refuse. Clear labeling, with pictures and/or graphics, can help to alleviate what goes in the landfill versus what is recycled or collected for reuse. Batteries of every kind, especially the coin cell lithium batteries common in many projects, require proper disposal for recycling and (along with e-waste) should never end up in landfills. Scraps and recycling are also fantastic sources for project materials, as we'll explore further in the "Materials & Tools" chapter.

POWER AND WATER

Proper power outlet planning and management is not just a matter of convenience, it's a matter of safety and fire code. Take the time to provide as many outlets as you can afford, and avoid the urge to string together extension cords and power strips. Over time, these solutions, often intended as temporary measures, become built-in, but they remain dangerous, unreliable, and unsafe, not to mention a violation of fire code.

Sinks are also important in makerspaces. We've known several makerspaces to be designed without them, and their absence, beyond just being a major inconvenience, can preclude many forms of making. Consider adding clay traps to all sinks, if possible, to capture particles and prevent major plumbing problems and expenses further down the road. Commercial clay traps are not cheap, but there are many DIY options available online developed by artists for home studios.

VENTILATION

Many forms of making are obvious in their requirements for ventilation, including soldering, woodworking with larger power tools, and using anything that releases volatile chemicals, such as glues with solvents or spray paint. Laser cutters absolutely require ventilation and may even require expensive filters, additional space and cost factors that must be considered when planning.

Something often forgotten is that all 3D printers require more ventilation than is commonly assumed. Recent studies have shown that 3D-printing plastic can emit high volumes of harmful ultrafine particles (UFP) that are as hazardous as cigarette smoke. These UFPs may not be obvious beyond a slight plastic smell. Bottom line: If you include a 3D printer in your space, you must consider adequate ventilation.

Larger woodworking tools often require dust-control systems and should ideally be housed in separate, dedicated areas, but the sawdust created by handsaws, in comparison, is easier to contain, enabling the tool to be used directly in a classroom environment. Smaller, portable power tools, such as circular and chop saws, might be brought outside if no dedicated indoor areas exist.

Furnishing for Everyone

We've heard this recommendation many times from spacemakers: when it comes to furniture, if you can put it on wheels, do so. Casters provide great flexibility and allow spaces to be adapted or even completely transformed in layout, according to needs. Mobile furniture can also make it easier to clean.

Many spaces have effectively invited the creation of furniture by youth as part of the experience. Shelves, tables, and chairs built from scratch can save a considerable amount of money and are a good way to invite community members and youth to contribute to the creation of a space. At the East Bay School for Boys in Berkeley, Calif., for example, students build their own desks, cubbies, and benches as a standard part of the curriculum. Many schools make good use of WikiSeats, an open-source design for an easily welded bracket standard that supports the creation of many varieties of stools.

Students in 10th and 11th grade at Scarsdale High School in New York prototyped furniture using cardboard, developing full-sized cardboard mockups to test the "feel" and functionality of the furniture. Initially designing and building in the classroom, they quickly spread the project into the halls and a gym when they began running out of space.

Photo: REM Learning Center

REM Learning Center's Play Make Share Studio

Program Director Ryan Moreno

"We've found ourselves continuously trying to strike a balance between scaffolded activities and open projects. Both approaches have aspects we consider as successful/powerful making. Creating classroom furniture with the children is one example of a successful scaffolded making activity. We work alongside children (ages four to nine) to design and make their own chairs for the Play Make Share Studio. A crucial element is removed from the classroom that many of the students take for granted: there will be something to sit on. To make this system function again for themselves and other classmates, they need to make chairs. They first look closely at the components that make up a chair and, as a group, design a chair for the space using an open-source chair as the foundation. It's an experience with a tangible result, where children are introduced to new tools while making a contribution to a system that will be used by others on a daily basis."

TABLES

Consider a variety of heights for working areas. Standing-height benches not only provide a healthier alternative to sitting, they can also save space by providing a work area that doesn't necessarily require stools to use. Low-level building areas can also save space, allowing makers to sit on the floor while they build. This is especially useful for young children or groups of mixed-aged makers, since any age can benefit from the utility of low building platforms. Regarding table heights and clearance around them, be sure to keep in mind table accommodation options for wheelchair users as well.

If designing tables from scratch, consider building in storage space under the table surfaces. Existing tables can also be adapted to provide these useful storage areas. At Pennsylvania's Millvale Community Library, because their space is used for multiple programs, they've designed tables that open up into storage space for sewing materials, with a working surface. At Miami's Play Make Share, tables have dry-erase tops for drawing, documenting, and visualizing thinking. The tables are also easily moveable, allowing for group discussions or for creating stations as needed for tasks.

Though you may choose to protect your table surfaces, many makerspaces celebrate the visible wear and tear. These surfaces take on character over time, capturing the history of making, a story in every mark and nick.

SHELVING

Shelves are incredibly important features in makerspaces. Visibility and organization are key. Open shelves are places where past projects and projects in-progress can be stored and displayed.

If certain tools need to be stored out of sight—in a cabinet, for example—provide a sign, picture, and/or symbol that makes the contents obvious. This is especially important for those too young to read and for non-native speakers. The overall goal is to make as many tools and materials visible, whether they are readily accessible or not.

Standalone shelving can also be used to help define and divide space, creating zones for various forms of making while still preserving line-of-site visibility. Shelving in many makerspaces is extensive, taking over entire walls; however, many of the simplest and most compact makerspaces are served by a single, well-stocked, logically planned bookshelf.

Phtoto:
Children's Museum
of Pittsburgh

TOOL WALLS AND CABINETS

A colorful student-made tool cabinet.
Photo: Analy High School

A dedicated tool wall, where the location of each tool is clearly defined with a label and outline of the tool, makes what is freely available visible and accessible. Alternately, tool cabinets can be constructed that expand upon opening yet still close for security and compartmentalization. Storage of tools and materials is among the biggest challenges of any makerspace. The *Makerspace Playbook: School Edition* has abundant examples of storage methods for tools and materials. We'll dive deeper into examples and methods of organizing efficiently and effectively in the next chapter on "Materials & Tools."

It's easy to get caught up in all the requirements for furniture, ventilation, tools, and materials in a space, as well as the complications they can create. It's always nice to be reminded that whenever you feel constrained by space, things can be made simpler. Young people come pre-equipped with all they need for meaningful making: ideas, interests, curiosity, and a love of creating and sharing stories. Materials, tools, and space can help enable these, but they can also overwhelm and hinder. Always consider the power of simply providing enough space and time for youth to gather, socialize, and play—making will invariably and naturally emerge in countless ways. ≡

Photo: Opal School

MATERIALS & TOOLS

While children have an innate ability to see the creative potential in just about anything, introducing new materials and tools can enable empowering experiences. That said, there's no denying that the materials and tools aspect of makerspaces can be daunting. The tendency to focus on what you don't have and what you think you need is especially common.

In this chapter, we concentrate on efficient, versatile, and inspiring materials and tools, many of which you likely already have or can easily obtain. We look at items that have most recently become favorites in many makerspaces (some of which may surprise you) as well as creative, affordable sources. Then, we examine the power of reusable materials, such as constructions sets, and look into methods of storage and issues of safety, all with an eye toward igniting new interests and providing transformative making experiences.

Art from reclaimed materials takes over the Bubbler with artist-in-resident Victor Castro.
Photo: Madison Public Library

Languages of Expression

Let's start by taking a moment to get philosophical about these physical objects. Much as the environment can be a "third teacher," materials and tools can be viewed as languages that enable expression, creation, and communication. Loris Malaguzzi's famous poem, "The 100 Languages of Children," speaks to the countless ways that children express themselves, through mediums such as visual arts, movement, music, dance, and basically anything that helps symbolically celebrate and share their thinking. He writes, "The child has a hundred languages, a hundred hands, a hundred thoughts, a hundred ways of thinking, of playing, of speaking."

Seen this way, materials and tools become a means not only to enable creating things but also to make visible the thoughts, feelings, and ideas of young makers. Makerspaces can provide opportunities for many forms of making and expression to come together, illuminating the youth's contributions to each other and to their communities. Their voices, their gifts—in the myriad of languages in which they're expressed—matter.

Maker Ed

Material Matters

What are some of the most "bang for the buck" materials? What are examples of common, efficient, and intelligent (read: adaptive, malleable) materials? Here's the great news: You likely already have some of the simplest and often most powerful materials on hand. Paper, water, sand/dirt/clay, blocks, dowels, scrap wood, arts and crafts materials, fabric and fibers, packing peanuts, bubble wrap, aluminum foil, and cardboard are all agents of awesome in the inventive hands of children.

We encourage you to begin by taking stock of what you already have available. What do you have that is consumable versus reusable? What will you need to restock (e.g., paper) and what can you get repeated use out of (e.g., blocks)? The planning sheet we introduced in "Getting Started" (available in Appendix A) is a handy resource to help you take stock. To expand your supplies list, let's consider some creative sources for materials that emphasize variety, utility, and affordability.

Photo: Maker Ed

OFFICE SUPPLIES

Binder clips, brads, paper clips, rubber bands, paper, and notebooks are readily available, inexpensive, and hold endless potential. Even the most mundane of materials can become fascinating and powerful depending on their invitation of use. Paper is a superstar in this realm: ubiquitous, versatile, and either taken for granted or incredibly creatively empowering, depending on how its use is invited. Having a wide variety of paper types on hand can allow for all sorts of creations and prototyping.

California-based Community Science Workshop Network is a prime example of operating under minimal material costs. They make extensive, clever use of common office supplies, which, when mixed in with other scrap and recycled materials, provide for countless projects and ways of exploring science concepts.

An office supply worth noting is the glue dot. These small, adhesive discs can take the place of hot glue in many circumstances. They come in several levels of strength and permanence. While not the cheapest, they allow for quick connections in the absence of glue guns.

When it comes to obtaining office supplies, local businesses sometimes have supplies they no longer need, so it's always worth asking.

SALVAGED AND RECYCLED

Many abundantly available materials, like cardboard and plastic bottles, are headed en masse to the recycling center or, sadly, to landfills. There are countless projects that can be made with recyclables, which come in an incredible array of novel shapes and sizes. This variety is especially useful for tinkering approaches (discussed in more detail in "Approaches & Practices"), which involve playing around with materials, seeking interesting ways to fit them together, and experimenting with forms and structures. Complete projects may or may not emerge, but the focus is on the process and seeking possibilities in the materials. For specific project ideas, check out Terracycle's wide selection of tutorials, which show how to make all manner of neat projects; pencil cases made from food pouch wrappers and chandeliers made of shampoo bottles are just two examples.

Making sure your makerspace has well-labeled trash and recycling receptacles is the first step toward collecting these useful materials. You can also check with your local recycling center to see if you can pick materials up. At Miami's Play Make Share makerspace, Friday is pizza day, so they started collecting the pizza box tops, and children use them to make open-ended laser-cut creations, like the dinosaur pictured, providing them a free, abundant prototyping material. Further, pizza boxes (or any cardboard or foamcore boards) can be combined with common office supplies to create simple circuits with no soldering required.

Roseville, Calif.-based ReCreate is entirely focused on encouraging the creation of art from reclaimed materials. Their message is "More art. Less waste." Founder Donna Sangwin elaborates, "We believe art and making should be accessible to anyone. To make that happen, we use nontraditional materials to get creative. Businesses have tons of great 'junk.' We use that to inspire creativity." ReCreate spends less than $3,000 per year on supplies to provide art experiences for 22,000 children annually.

Photo:
REM Learning Center

When looking for streams from which to salvage materials, don't forget construction sites. Wood, cardboard, and PVC pipe are among the common leftover materials of building construction. Cabinet shops are also a great potential source for wood scraps. Leftover political campaign signs made of corrugated plastic are yet another abundant and useful material. Always ask permission to salvage, but folks are often happy to donate what they would otherwise throw away, especially knowing the materials have potential to help children grow and learn.

DONATED, SECOND-HAND, AND SURPLUS

You never know what materials members of your community may have to donate until you put the word out. The Millvale Community Library makerspace has received many useful donations by soliciting online as well as posting physical flyers. They also look to estate sales to find second-hand tools for their tool-lending library.

Photo:
Children's Museum
of Pittsburgh

The Children's Museum of Pittsburgh's Makeshop gets all kinds of interesting donations, the most memorable of which has been two garbage bags full of Dictaphones (dictation machines). This led to all kinds of creative projects, the most surprising of which was making use of the abundant, very fine, colorful electrical wires salvaged from the Dicatophone cords for weaving in looms.

Photo: ReCreate

Play Make Share asks participating families to donate their outdated and broken electronics and toys for activities that involve disassembly and exploration. They also collect cardboard tubes, useful in a variety of projects, from local printing companies, carpet dealers, and architectural firms.

Thrift stores are another great source of inexpensive project materials. STEAMLabs cites second-hand toys as being particularly useful, noting that children take them apart and use them for a variety of projects. STEAMLabs also uses their local surplus store as a steady source of affordable materials. Likewise, CoLab Tinkering's summer camp and workshops have made extensive use of materials gathered at Goodwill outlet stores, where craft and art supplies, old electronic toys, and all sorts of incredibly useful items can be bought for less than a dollar per pound.

PROJECT SCRAPS

Much of what might be considered "waste" in making can either be recycled or be valuable to reuse and inspire new projects. Often, a trimmed piece of fabric or cut end of a block of wood might be the perfect part for a new project. A scrap piece of plastic or a wire could provide the ideal inspiration for new creations. Clearly labeling scrap bins by general material type helps provide variety, inspiration, and convenience of use.

At the Free Library of Philadelphia's Maker Jawn program, one of their Maker Mentors, Lauren Rodriguez, came up with The Sculpture Challenge, a creative activity that uses up various knickknacks and scraps that accumulate in their space. She places random items in envelopes and hands them to participants, who then have to use all the pieces to create a sculpture.

Photos:
Free Library of Philadelphia

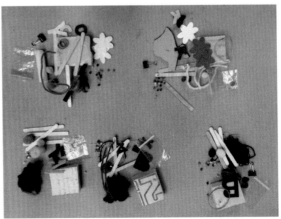

CONSTRUCTION SETS

Stocking up on construction sets is an investment in reuse. The varieties of sets that exist, as well as their resounding popularity, are testament to the fact that they not only ignite the imagination but also support prototyping, serving as initial points of inspiration, ideation, and experimentation.

One of the affordances of these building systems is that they provide an easy invitation to build and play. Young children, especially, show us that through play, stories naturally emerge. More than just construction materials, they can be story platforms. Construction sets can also help effectively build social-emotional skills, such as learning to share resources and care for materials.

We've put together a chart to look at the affordances of four different construction sets (see Appendix C). There are tons of sets available, but these are among the best that have withstood the test of time and provide a huge range of engagement and possibilities.

We encourage you to explore ways of expanding these systems with other materials, such as paper, and electronic components. For example, an economical way to add electromechanical complexity is the addition of salvaged motors and batteries. You need not rely on the "official" brand-specific motor elements, which can be very expensive. A great challenge is to adapt hobby DC motors to provide movement. LEDs can also be added to each system.

For the plank systems, plastic Brackitz (formerly Bionic Blox) are available to provide an additional building method, turning the block, friction, and balance system into struts and connectors, increasing their adaptability and affordances. A nice role for 3D printing has been the creation of many adaptors, like the Free Universal Construction Kit, designed to enable these and other building systems to work together.

Don't be shy about "breaking the rules" of a particular construction system. Combinations, extra material additions, and modifications can be very inspiring and provide all kinds of unexpected possibilities beyond the original design intentions. Employ whatever it takes to make the best use of what you have. Playing within the rules, as a form of creative constraint, can inspire as well. You win either way. Happy building!

Photo: Maker Ed

Maker Ed

Making with mud. Photo:
New York Hall of Science

NATURAL MATERIALS

Think of any child turned loose to play in the woods, a park, a backyard, or on the beach. Chances are it won't be long before they start gathering materials and creating things with them. Primordial materials like mud, sticks, leaves, rocks, sand, and water, abundant in quantity, offer potential for materials exploration, free play, or planning and constructing. With the right framing, a pile of sticks and leaves can become stacks of construction material for a collaborative shelter build. How might you leverage the power of natural materials in your space? How might you take making outside?

Trees can become climbing structures, places for forts, and may even create art. Loose materials, leaves, stones, pinecones, twigs, and petals become materials for collages or can be mixed with blocks for increased building possibilities. Sticks can be lashed together to create strong structures.

Garden spaces can teach the art of growing and making food, and fostering plants indoors may invite time-lapse movies tracking growth from seed germination onward. Hydroponics projects allow for learning about plant nutrition and growing with more efficient water use.

A whole world of projects and explorations becomes possible when wind, sunlight, and water become materials to play and build with. What projects might you create that make use of the sun, such as solar cookers or sundials? Sunlight can even be brought inside using mirrors and prisms. Wind invites power generation and creations such a kinetic sculptures or kites that playfully move and respond to it. Fans can be used indoors to capture this spirit.

With careful consideration about what is gathered and in what quantities, nature provides a vast construction set and offers an exercise in using natural resources carefully and sustainably. Before gathering materials outdoors, discuss what might be collected in reasonable quantities without harm (loose twigs, leaves, pinecones) and what should not be gathered (breaking limbs off trees). Children can help lead the way in establishing rules for responsible use of natural materials and in doing so build greater sensitivity toward issues of sustainability.

Photos:
Opal Beginning School of the
Portland Children's Museum

Tools

Great tools not only unlock the potential of materials, they provide an empowering extension of self and creativity. Consider what your favorite tools are and why. Likely, your favorites are such due to what they've allowed you to do or how they've made you feel when using them. Perhaps driving a nail with a hammer felt a bit dangerous but satisfying, or the feeling of melting metal while soldering or welding was particularly exciting. From knitting needles to musical instruments, programming languages to cooking utensils, favorite tools "speak" to those who discover and love them. What potential favorite tools might you introduce?

There's a useful, basic makerspace tools list in the *Makerspace Playbook: School Edition*, which includes tools for joining, fixturing, cutting, electronics, textiles, and more. As much as that list can be helpful to get your wheels turning, there's no *prescribed* set of tools that defines a makerspace. Instead of focusing on what tools you *should* have, consider what types of making your space will initially support. Start simple and add tools as the needs of your community become apparent and your programming develops. In this section, we look at a variety of popular tools, ranging greatly in complexity but all sharing the power to transform materials and provide varieties of making and expression.

THE MIGHTY GLUE GUN

Of the makerspace site surveys that we conducted, there was no singular tool more loved than the humble but mighty glue gun. This is a true super tool. At Play Make Share, a makerspace for ages four to nine years old, Ryan Moreno says, "The hot glue gun has been the most useful, sought-after, and versatile tool for all ages. For children, using the hot glue gun is a transformative experience: pom-poms, feathers, and any other material can be hot-glued and transformed into anything from wings to passengers. Scissors would probably be a close second favorite, followed by screwdrivers and hammers."

One of the best ways to help keep hot glue gun use safe is to emphasize using small amounts of hot glue. Burns often come from large, dripping globs of hot glue that are more excessive than they need to be. Ventilation is helpful to minimize the plastic smell, but at least hot glue lacks the toxic solvents, the volatile organic compounds (VOCs), of many liquid glues. Having clear signage with usage tips is helpful for any tool. A highly visible indicator of when the power is on, like a lit power switch, also helps prevent accidents.

Photo:
REM Learning Center

Of course we can't talk about glue guns without mentioning the heat gun. Heat guns are like industrial-strength hair dryers and offer a variety of uses, such as loosening hot-glued parts and shrinking heat-shrink tubing, used to strengthen electrical and mechanical connections. Heat guns are also useful for stripping chipped paint as well as drying paint to facilitate applying multiple layers.

Maker Ed

TRADITIONAL TOOLS

In the wake of the popularity of digital fabrication tools, traditional tools still hold transformative power: hammers, screwdrivers, drills, saws, scissors, sewing machines, basic sewing supplies, knitting needles, pottery wheels, screen-printing tools, punches, eyelet setters, and more. Attaching one thing to another, whether it's fabric with thread or wood pieces with nails, is still a powerful making experience. Being able to weave your own cloth on a loom is still inspiring (a paper loom is easy to make). The Omaha Children's Museum even turned their entire makerspace into a loom for a week.

Simple tools can also be modified for more impact. For example, inexpensive jigsaw blades, broken in half with the ends wrapped in duct tape, make the best cardboard saws. Further, be sure to consider all kinds of tools, not just the ones that are associated with workshops. For example, readily available kitchen tools, like rolling pins and potato mashers, have many uses beyond the kitchen.

SHOP TOOLS FOR EVERYONE

Given the abundance of information available on traditional shop tools, we'll use this opportunity to emphasize the potential of simple hand tools. There's something very powerful about shaping materials by hand. Bottom line: Don't fear handsaws, power drills, and other hand tools. Respect them and imagine what the simplest of tools has achieved throughout the history of humanity. Too often, tools are presented to young people as something that can't be touched and aren't for them. Your invitations to use simple hand tools are nothing short of empowering.

For example, there's a great simple satisfaction in nailing and driving screws. Hammers can be a perfect place to start, with something as simple as driving a nail into a large stump or block of wood. Pre-drill a bunch of small holes of various sizes in a block of wood or soft plastic (polyoxymethylene, aka Delrin, works particularly well) and watch even the youngest of makers spend tons of time driving in and out screws of various sizes with hand or powered screwdrivers. It's these real tools, the same that might be used by any adult, that make strong impressions in their use.

Photo: DIY Girls

At the Children's Museum of Pittsburgh's Makeshop, Lisa Brahms shares, "Tools and materials are selected to be functional, while taking into consideration the size, strength, and skill levels of our visitors. For example, all of the hammers in Makeshop are capable of driving nails. There are no plastic versions available, but there may be an assortment of handle lengths or grip styles, in order to best match the tools with the individual needs and skills of the user."

Sometimes a tool ends up not being a good match for everyone. At STEAMLabs, Andy Forest says, "Our table saw is mostly used by the adult mentors. It's just too powerful and the potential for kickback too strong. We're looking into getting a wall-mounted panel saw to replace it as a more kid-friendly tool."

When cutting, drilling, or gluing things together, don't forget the vices and clamps. Effective ways to fix and hold materials are absolutely essential for safety. For great general woodworking tips, check out this intro and these resources.

3D PRINTERS

There's no shortage of information on this ever-growing area of making, so we won't go into too much detail here. Instead, we'll give you permission to not need one. Certainly, 3D printers can be exciting and powerful, enabling children to bring digital designs into the physical realm. They can also be always broken, a bottleneck, and an extra expense. For example, Makeshop's 3D printers often sit unused because the upkeep and adjustments outweighed the time they've chosen to devote to them. As Lisa Brahms shares, they place a higher priority on "supporting young children's engagement with tactile tools and materials, and the time necessary to print objects is not well-suited to the ways in which young children engage in our space."

Use is a question involving several factors, including age and priorities. When these align, 3D printer use can be integral to the space. At the Children's Museum of Houston, the 3D printers are by far the most popular tools, followed by the laser cutter. In a particularly ambitious project, a group of middle school students built a 3D printer from a kit and donated the printer to their school.

Photo:
Children's Museum
of Houston

For Baltimore's Digital Harbor Foundation, a high priority is supporting youth-led 3D-printing entrepreneurial efforts. Through their Perpetual Innovation Fund, students and educators submit business plans detailing how they would use 3D printers to create and sell products and/or services. If selected, they receive a 3D printer, training, and mentorship, and they commit to giving initial profits back to the fund to support other youth enterprises.

Regardless of your priorities, if you do have a 3D printer, there will be a segment of your learners that are very excited about the possibilities of running and maintaining the machine. This can be very empowering. Imagine students teaching teachers the finer points of printing or youth mentors providing guidance for library patrons on 3D design and printing. No doubt it's an exciting area. It can be a youth-centered one as well.

FURTHER FAB TOOLS

Aside from 3D printers, other digital fabrication tools, like laser cutters, vinyl cutters, and CNC mills, have the makersphere abuzz. Once solely the realm of professionals, these tools have become more accessible, in cost as well as barrier to entry, to the hobbyist.

Maker Ed

In 2005, Saul Griffith wrote "The Maker's Ultimate Tools," outlining a master tool list, ranging from basic to extreme high-end, complete with associated costs. Eight years later, James Floyd Kelly referenced Griffith's piece in his article "Kickstart a Kids' Makerspace," distilling the list to focus on fab tools for kids. To the vast existing information that addresses these tools, we simply emphasize the importance of budgeting for the filters, ventilation, upkeep, and training necessary to maximize the use of these tools in a children's makerspace.

Similar to 3D printers, our site surveys show that while digital fabrication tools appear on the favorites list of some spaces, they often sit collecting dust at other spaces due to complexity and how time-consuming the processes can be. Choose and plan wisely by considering the factors mentioned above and researching thoroughly, ensuring the existence of necessary skills and support by users, as well as the proper computer and software support. For all things involving digital fabrication, the Fab Foundation, an educational outreach of MIT's Center for Bits and Atoms, is an excellent resource.

TOOLS FOR CAPTURING AND SHARING

Sharing knowledge is one of the cornerstones of makerspaces across the board, so we would be remiss to not mention the tools of documentation. Tools like video and audio recording equipment, cameras, and computers provide the means not only for children to document their work to share with their peers and the larger community but also for makerspace organizers to share their methods, projects, and progress with the makerspace community. Everyone wins with documentation. Additionally, for the youth, documenting their work helps lend an empowering sense of ownership and accomplishment, as well as offering a unique opportunity for reflection.

A staff-created
DIY documentation station.
Photo: Digital Harbor Foundation

One interesting example of facilitating documentation is at DIY Girls, where they've created a "Maker Talk" booth that has been successful in getting the girls to talk about their making experiences. The booth is hidden away in a corner or behind a curtain with no adult supervision. Girls sit in front of the camera and answer questions provided, which include: What project did you work on today? Did you have any challenges? What are you most proud of? What do you want to make next?

Documentation tools help capture and celebrate the people behind the space. In a powerful statement, Trent Miller of the Madison Public Library's Bubbler makerspace, says, "We prioritize people over equipment. While we do have a media lab with amazing technology that was created with our start-up grant, moving forward, we would rather pay artists to share their skills than to invest in equipment."

The tools of capturing process, thinking, and projects are important to keep in mind when outfitting your makerspace. We delve into much greater detail about documentation in the "Sustainability" chapter and cover some methods in Appendix E.

Exploring Electronics

Electronics as a form of making is one very often associated with the modern Maker Movement. It seems that anything with LEDs, motors, microcontrollers, or code enjoys a very high profile. It's true these areas are exciting and powerful. They can also be new and intimidating, not to mention expensive. What are some materials and tools that can help anyone discover the properties of components such as motors, LEDs, and batteries?

Three Circuit Exploration Tools

There are many products to buy (or make) for exploring electricity and electronic circuits. Let's look at three tested champions.

Photo:
Children's Museum
of Pittsburgh

Circuit Blocks

Circuit blocks are a set of components, switches, and power sources that can be tethered together, making electronics exploration easy and safe. They have all sorts of features and benefits: they're affordable, expandable, transparent, endlessly customizable, and can be made right there in your makerspace. Makeshop offers a great tutorial.

Squishy Circuits

Developed by AnnMarie Thomas, this fun, accessible, and inexpensive way to explore circuits makes use of conductive and non-conductive (insulating) dough. Children can make their own Squishy Circuits using components such as batteries and LEDs.

Breadboards

This prototyping mainstay, along with jumper wires and various electronic components, enables authentic experimentation but for less cost than actually soldering the components onto a board. Components can be used over and again. Maker Ed has created a guide for introducing young makers to physical computing, which features a section on breadboards.

Photo: Maker Ed

There's no denying the sheer joy that young makers (and adults!) experience when they first learn to solder, complete their first circuit, or do something as simple as make an LED light up. Suddenly the mysterious world of electronics becomes accessible, and a whole universe of project opportunity opens up to them.

New and powerful computational tools are being made available at a pace that's often hard to keep up with. The Arduino microcontroller was developed in 2005 as an inexpensive and accessible microcontroller for makers of all stripes. Since then, the options have multiplied exponentially. Adafruit's mini microcontroller, called Trinket, retails for $6. Further, the Raspberry Pi is essentially a single-board mini computer that retails for as little as $25.

A favorite electronics-learning tool among makerspaces is Makey Makey, which enables users to connect everyday objects, such as fruit, vegetables, and themselves, to computer programs using a circuit board, alligator clips, and a USB cable. A classic sample project is making a banana piano and playing the fruit like an instrument. In their site survey, Albuquerque's OLÉ actually listed the Makey Makey (along with bananas and broccoli) as being among the most popular tools at their makerspace. Beyond the use of fruit and vegetables, much can be discovered by taking advantage of the conductive properties of plants, pencil drawings, tinfoil, water, and more. Ample examples can be found online, but leaving room for discovery and invention can be even more powerful.

Maker Ed

On the software side, a favorite introduction to programming is Scratch, the free authoring tool developed by the Lifelong Kindergarten Group at MIT Media Lab. Young makers can use Scratch (often paired with MaKey Makey) to create their own computer-based games, affording a first foray into the power of coding. Scratch also has a robust site with endless project ideas and a large, active community. For more advanced approaches, Processing and Python are popular, free, and open-source programming languages.

Tinkering with and exploring electronics need not be expensive. A lot can be done with simple and salvaged materials. A perennial tinkering activity is taking apart old electronics, which can be acquired either inexpensively or freely (see Appendix B for guidance). Children learn a great deal about objects by being given the license to take them apart, without the restrictive fear of breaking something.

As well, some inexpensive, everyday objects hold potential for tinkering with electronics. Brent Richardson of the Children's Museum of Houston advises, "Anything that can conducts electricity can have surprising applications. Pipe cleaners, for instance, can be used in circuits and produce interesting results. Additional conductive materials include washers, nails, foil, and graphite."

Safety

Naturally, the standard implements of safety, such as eye protection, first aid supplies, and fire extinguishers, are necessary in any makerspace. But equally as important is clear and abundant communication. When the groundwork of acceptable behavior and tool use is clearly laid out and reinforced using signage, there's less room for misunderstanding, mitigating the chance of accidents.

INTRODUCING TOOLS AND MATERIALS

Understanding the affordances of tools and materials—namely, how they work, what they make possible, and their strengths and limitations—is of critical importance for their safe use. The right tool or material for any given job isn't just the most effective—it's the safest.

Safe tool use begins with conversation. When introducing a tool and material for the first time, it's helpful to include learners in the discussion. Ask questions to spur discussion. What do you notice about the tool/material? What do you wonder about it? What can it be used for? What might go wrong? In this way, understanding and agreements about proper and safe use can be built collaboratively with youth, establishing shared ownership and investment. Resulting conversations may sound like, "It's cool you can melt things with the soldering iron. I'll bet it could hurt, too. Can it set paper on fire? Does it stay hot after I'm done with it? How can I let people know that it's still hot when I'm done?"

Many makerspaces establish that all tools, from hammers to laser cutters, require training before being free to use without adult supervision. Even trainings can be designed to be youth-centered. At STEAMLabs, for example, when a new tool is introduced, the facilitator leads a conversation about the right tool for the job, followed by a conversation about how to use the tool. For the second time a child uses a tool, instead of telling them the rules for the tool again, children are encouraged to teach another child how to use the tool, with a mentor listening.

Photo: STEAMLabs

Photos: DIY Girls

SIGNAGE AND CONTRACTS

Signs can provide helpful on-the-spot instruction and reminders throughout your space. At DIY Girls, each piece of equipment has an instructional sign on the wall next to it promoting safe usage. There is also a contract, which outlines the rules and agreements of the space, that each of the girls who uses the space signs. The verbiage of the contract is also posted on the wall as a reminder. We'll let these signage examples speak for themselves.

Organizing It All

Now that you have the space, the tools, and the materials, how do you organize it all, maximize your storage space, and make it all accessible at the same time? Each makerspace has to develop a unique system that works with their actual space and usage patterns, but by and large, many use bins and simple classification systems, sorting and labeling according to type of material (wood, plastic, metal) or activity (soldering, sewing, painting).

At STEAMLabs, for instance, in an effort to keep their central space as open, malleable, and multipurpose as possible, they've developed "Tool Pods" that have everything you need for a particular activity, like soldering, and slide out on to your workbench, ready to start.

At Lighthouse Community Charter School's Creativity Lab, materials and tools are organized neatly in labeled bins on shelves. Materials that are not used regularly are stored in closets. The team collaborates on reorganizing the space once a month.

In the Maker Jawn program of the Free Library of Philadelphia, which is hosted at five different neighborhood libraries, Sarah Winchowsky shares, "We generally use a lot of boxes and bins since designated shelving is often not available. At some sites, we've worked with program participants to organize and label the storage of tools and materials. This is helpful in getting everyone familiar with where things are located as well as in giving people a sense of ownership and pride of the space."

At The Bubbler makerspace in the Madison Public Library, the majority of their art supplies are available for the public to use. They have a collection of old card catalog drawers that they've labeled and filled with scissors, markers, crayons, glue, etc.

Maker Ed

What materials can I use to make my project?

Non-Consumable Prototyping Material
1) Do not cut, glue, or paint it.
2) You can not keep it.
3) Does not leave the Makerspace without permission.

Semi-Consumable Prototyping Material
1) Get permission use & to cut, glue, and paint it.
2) Get permission to keep it.
3) Does not leave the Makerspace without permission.

Consumable Prototyping Material
1) Cut it, glue it, paint it!
2) Yours to keep
3) Ask for guidance when using in large quantities

Photo:
Chadwick International School

As an alternative system for material organization, Marymount School in New York organizes according to type of activity rather than material or project types. Instead of labeling "Electronics" or "Sewing," for instance, fab lab coordinator Jaymes Dec has their shelves and bins arranged by such labels as "Invent Something" or "Prototype Something."

Teacher Andrew Carle of Chadwick International school in Incheon, South Korea, includes a color-coded system that classifies materials based on the question "What materials can I use to make my project?"

However organized your materials might be, as long as the message is clear that options exist and a range of materials and tools are freely accessible, you're on the right track. Clutter will always be a factor, no matter the system. Whatever your comfort level might be with it, many makerspaces embrace a degree of chaos in the midst of order. After all, it shows authentic and dynamic use of the space.

As with all aspects of a makerspace, tools, materials, safety agreements, and organization should be hinged upon and become a reflection of the heart of the space. The most effective tools and materials will be ones that are inspired by the interests of the users and are introduced by those using and/or supporting the space, including makers of all kinds from the wider community.

When people's passions and interests drive the material and tool selections, things become more personal, and that energy is contagious. Perhaps an artist will introduce paints and easels, as well as model a love of art and provide mentorship. Any number of hobbyists, artisans, gamers, athletes, musicians, and chefs might bring the materials and tools of their trades into your space, thereby igniting new interests. Our hope is that by sharing the examples in this chapter and encouraging you to consider the capabilities and resources abundant in your space and community, your own wheels are turning. Are you sketching your ideas? ≡

Photo: CoLab Tinkering

APPROACHES & PRACTICES

hus far we've addressed the tangible aspects of creating a
makerspace: the physical space itself, the tools, and the materials.
ust as there are a myriad of environments that can enable and
ncourage making, there are multiple mindsets and pedagogies
hat can be applied to makerspaces.

In this chapter, we begin by offering a general overview of the approaches
and learning theories most common in maker education. Along the way, we
highlight concrete examples of how established makerspaces have combined
these ideas to develop their own unique styles. We'll only be scratching the
surface here, so if any of the ideas discussed resonate with you, we encourage
you to delve deeper using the links throughout or by visiting our Resource
Library. In the second half of the chapter, we explore the application of these
ideas to the facilitation of making experiences for youth. We touch on various
points of entry to consider, the role of youth and adults, and the ways that
language can be used to inspire creativity.

Learning Approaches

In addition to promoting learning through hands-on activity, maker education
puts particular emphasis on re-evaluating the roles of students and facilitators.
At the core is the learner, posing questions, experimenting, and developing
ideas, rather than simply being fed information and knowledge. Below is an
overview of four commonly used approaches, each of which offers a unique
angle and emphasis.

 discussion of approaches in maker education would be complete
thout mentioning the foundational contributions of American
ilosopher, psychologist, and educational reformist John Dewey
859–1952). One of his famous quotes, which succinctly summarizes
s views on education, reads, "Give the pupils something to do, not
mething to learn; and the doing is of such a nature as to demand
inking; learning naturally results."

Photo:
Used with permission from
the University of Chicago
Library Special Collections.

INQUIRY-BASED MAKING AND LEARNING

As the name implies, inquiry-based learning
starts with questions posed, rather than
facts given. Learners are encouraged to
develop their own questions and consider
projects, experiments, and explorations
that can help them reach conclusions,
create solutions, and/or convey ideas.
Academically, inquiry approaches apply
to all subject areas. In STEM fields, inquiry
methods complement the scientific method
and greatly enrich investigations in math,
engineering, and technology.

Maker Ed

Wind-powered artbots.
Photo: Opal School

A micro-watercolor
artbot using Q-tips.
Photo: Maker Ed

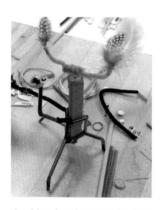

A rubber-band-powered artbot.
Photo: Maker Ed

Photo:
Free Library of Philadelphia

The National Science Teachers Association outlines the following four levels of inquiry. To put the approach in concrete context, we use the project example of artbots, simple electromechanical creations that make art.

○ **Confirmational:** Students are taught a concept, then posed a question and given an experiment/project/activity that will lead them to the concept they learned, confirming and solidifying their new knowledge. Example: The facilitator may be teaching about electrical circuits, demonstrate how an offset weight on the shaft of a DC motor creates a shaking motion, and show how a specific kind of artbot makes use of this motion to move and draw with markers. Learners are then asked to build an artbot using instructions, an example, or kits. Through the build, the circuit and mechanical concepts they've seen demonstrated are reproduced, solidifying the concepts.

○ **Structured:** The facilitator poses a question and outlines an experiment, project, challenge, or area of investigation, and then learners respond. Example: The facilitator may ask, "How does the position of the shaking motor change how the artbot draws?" Learners are then invited to investig how different motor positions, balance, and weight distribution change behavior and to make note of the changes and effects.

○ **Guided:** The facilitator only poses questions, or even just a broad project genre and the students are responsible for devising a project and/or experiment to explore the question or challenge. Example: The facilitator may simply ask, "In what ways might these materials make and/or become art?" The learners would then tinker, build, and experiment to create their own designs, guided by the material selection options and the challenge to create art. The facilitator may suggest possible approaches, designs, or provide examples for inspiration, but these are not meant to be replicated literally.

○ **Open:** Students devise their own questions, projects, experiments, and evaluations/conclusions. Example: Only materials to choose from are made available along with an open-ended (though still slightly guiding) invitation to explore and discover, such as "What is possible with these materials? What kin of things can they do?" Artbots in various forms may arise from tinkering and a made possible by material selection, but specific examples are not shown at the beginning and the materials themselves serve as the inspiration and challenge for what's possible. As tinkering and work progresses, examples of all types of projects naturally arise throughout the process, rather than being prompted or provided specifically by the facilitator.

Some young makers enthusiastically run with open-ended invitations, while others have greater comfort with more concrete and structured starting points. Having examples on hand that are only selectively shared can help honor this spectrum of comfort. For instance, to help alleviate any possible anxiety, the facilitator might let students know that there are examples to share in the case that someone feels truly stuck. Often, the "safety net" of examples is not even needed as comfort levels increase with the knowledge that help and inspiration are readily available.

Inquiry-based explorations and project work blend multiple forms of inquiry. A structured demonstration of a motor's use may inspire open-ended explorations. Open inquiry creations may provide examples for future guided or structured approaches.

PROJECT-BASED LEARNING

Just as it sounds, project-based learning (PBL) centers on facilitating meaningful, powerful learning experiences through project work and the context that projects provide for learning.

According to nonprofit foundation Edutopia, the five keys to PBL are:

o   **Establish real-world connections in projects.** Start with an authentic problem, need, or opportunity in the community and anchor the learning with a driving question.

o   **Build projects that are core to learning.** In schools, projects and standards can easily coexist, where projects anchor the curriculum and enable students to apply and practice their knowledge.

o   **Structure collaboration for student success.** Choreograph collaboration by helping students develop roles/responsibilities and processes, teaching them how to use each other as resources.

o   **Facilitate learning in a student-driven environment.** Introduce the topic in a way that promotes curiosity, allowing students to find their own answers or generate more questions. Make time for reflection and have students track their own progress.

o   **Embed assessment throughout the project.** Because projects can span weeks, build in mini learning targets to assess, not just by the educator but also by the students themselves and the group as a whole. End with a presentation or performance.

Often, concrete projects are used as a step towards learning a technical skill, familiarizing oneself with tools, or becoming more adept at tackling larger and more individualized projects. For example, educators have prompted students to "make a pillow." Innate to this project is the development of sewing skills and familiarity with sewing tools and materials, along with application of math and measurements. Pillows take on forms of their own: youth (in pairs or groups) may create body pillows, dog beds, pillows for homeless shelters, travel pillows, seat cushions, or pillows with lights and sensors.

While PBL is naturally focused on projects, it's complemented well by approaches that emphasize process, such as playing, exploring, and tinkering, where creating a finished product isn't a goal. And though PBL curricula tends to focus on real-world situations as the inspiration for projects, youth-derived projects based purely on whimsy or individual interests can also provide valuable learning experiences with personal meaning.

Photo:
Opal School/ CoLab Tinkering

TINKERING

At the core of the tinkering philosophy is a playful celebration of discovery through inquiry, exploration, prototyping, and iterating. It has been said that play is a child's most serious work. Powerful learning opportunities are present when children are allowed to pose their own questions and devise methods for exploring possible outcomes. According to the Exploratorium's book *The Art of Tinkering*, tenets include:

- Be comfortable not knowing.
- Prototype rapidly.
- Balance autonomy with collaboration.
- Use familiar materials in unfamiliar ways.
- Express ideas via construction.
- Revisit and iterate on ideas.
- Put yourself in messy situations.
- Seek real-world examples everywhere.

For a deeper look at tinkering, read the comprehensive paper entitled "Designing for Tinkerability" by Mitchel Resnick and Eric Rosenbaum of MIT's Lifelong Kindergarten group. They summarize the key lessons they've learned from designing contexts for tinkerability:

- Emphasize process over product.
- Set themes, not challenges.
- Highlight diverse examples.
- Tinker with [physical] space.
- Encourage engagement with people not just materials.
- Pose questions instead of giving answers.
- Combine diving in with stepping bac

Photo: CoLab Tinkering

STEAMLabs: Blended Approach Based on PBL and Tinkering

**Chief Instigator
Andy Forest**

Photo: STEAMLabs

Our main method of teaching is experiential and interest-driven. Play-based learning is also very important. Our five-step process is as follows:

1. **Explore technology.** Discover something new by experimenting with it. We provide multiple options. This frequently involves taking things apart to see how they work.

2. **Brainstorm ideas.** Think of interesting and useful ways to use technology to make something. Inspired by the exploration and play step, participants can now let their imaginations run wild and come up with ideas.

3. **Make a plan.** Grab some team members an turn your idea into a plan you can execute together. Understand that people have differen strengths, and a team is much greater than the sum of its parts. This step first involves selectiv retention of the ideas formed in the previous st Refine this into a plan that can be accomplishe

4. **Build, fail, repeat.** Get to work on your crea Learning how to overcome problems is the be way to learn. We guide participants to solve the own problems and get used to being self-relia

5. **Success!** Celebrate your creation by sharing and your process (more important than the fin product) through journals and presentations.

Sample Project: A grade six class designed and built an Internet of Things (IoT) interactive model of Ontario's power system as a museum exhibit to teach about power generation and consumption. This is more than a school project; it's an actual educational installation piece. The finished model was accepted into an exhibit at the Toronto International Film Festival's Digiplayspace.

DESIGN THINKING

Like other design and engineering processes, design thinking often focuses on the stages and process through which a solution is created. With design thinking, these modes include empathize, define, ideate, prototype, and test. At its very core, though, utmost importance is placed on the fact that this methodology is human-centered: clarity comes from developing empathy for and understanding the needs of the user(s). Some compare it, as a parallel, to the scientific method, where one might have a problem, come up with a hypothesis, and experiment to test it. With design thinking, the problem isn't obvious or clear until one engages with a broad range of users to understand their needs and insights.

According to Stanford University's d.school, the main principles are as follows:
o   **Human-Centered:** Respond to human needs and user feedback.
o   **Mindful of Process:** Be mindful not only of what is being made but also of the specific process used to make, with attention to how the process can be improved.
o   **Culture of Prototyping:** Value experimenting and quickly iterating based on what is learned in the process.
o   **Bias Toward Action:** Be in favor of trying things out over discussing possible outcomes.
o   **Show Don't Tell:** Value expressing ideas visually (sketching, prototyping, digital storytelling), knowing it brings issues and opportunities to light.
o   **Radical Collaboration:** Sharing every step of a process can help highlight individual team member strengths and increase the skill sets of the group as a whole, as well as facilitate bringing together people of vastly different skill sets and backgrounds.

In maker education, especially with projects that respond to a community need, design thinking can be incorporated in the beginning stages. Youth have an opportunity to practice their observation and interviewing techniques, uncover insights, distill their findings, and brainstorm possibilities. The actual users themselves can even affirm the final solution; if it satisfies, the work has made a real impact.

oto:
ildren's Museum
Houston

Maker Ed

For further reading, delve into the d.school's active toolkit, which provides a deeper overview of the modes of design thinking, as well as numerous concrete methods.

New York Hall of Science (NYSCI): Blended Approach Based on Design Thinking

Director of Early Childhood Education Janella Watson

We aim to root each of our workshops, the environment we create, and the learning experiences we provide for families in NYSCI's Design Make Play pedagogy. The core ingredients we believe make Design Make Play transformative experiences for STEM learning for young children and their families are as follows:

Materials Literacy: When children are able to find new uses for everyday materials, they develop materials literacy, a potent skill that enables children to see possibilities in the world around them.

Science Process Skills and Engaging in Mathematical Thinking: Making experiences rooted in deep noticing afford open-ended ways to understand the world through asking questions, probing for answers, investigating, and communicating. By providing natural phenomena to explore and the tools to investigate them, making encourages the development of skills including identification and creation of patterns, measurement, counting, sorting, and classification—skills at the core of early mathematical thinking.

Purposeful Play: We make sense of our world through self-directed, rich, sensory experiences. Play develops children's content knowledge and provides them the opportunity to develop social skills, competences, and disposition to learn.

Divergent Solutions: We nurture children's natural creativity through experiences that are open-ended and invite learners to define their own paths, rooted in what excites them and makes them curious. Making inspires learners to approach materials and processes in new and innovative ways, reflective of their own creative thinking, gives ownership over what they create, and encourages kids to be natural problem solvers.

Collaboration and Co-learning: By highlighting the opportunity for math and science learning in children's everyday experiences, and elaborating on the science that families are already doing together, we both provide meaningful ways for adults to participate in making and encourage continued experimentation at home.

Documentation and Sharing: For young learners, who build confidence and agency through self-expression, sharing is at the heart of their healthy socio-emotional development. Opportunities for storytelling, muraling, and sketching, paired with physical displays and digital documentation of children's work, acknowledge and support children's desires to communicate and represent their knowledge of the world as well as inspire further investigation and exploration.

Sample Projects (from the Little Makers program):
Bird Nesting: Birds have unique ways of using special materials to make their homes. Explore the science behind nest making and transform recycled materials into a nest of your own. Wood Works: Practice woodworking skills as you learn to measure, drive nails with a hammer, and use sandpaper. Then design and create wooden projects such as racecars and birdhouses.

As you may have noticed, there are many similarities between these four approaches. To name a few, they are all student-centered, include multiple pathways for the learner to explore, focus on process, and emphasize "question asking" over "question answering." And while each approach can be used purely on its own, they can also be blended and tailored to suit the unique flavor of your makerspace.

**earning
heories**

Another similarity between the learning approaches we explored is their application of two foundational learning theories. Because constructivism and constructionism are terms that get tossed around a lot in maker education, we thought it important to take a brief moment to introduce them, differentiate between them, and spark your curiosity to delve deeper.

CONSTRUCTIVISM

Formally developed by Jean Piaget in the first half of the 20th century, constructivism is a cognitive theory that claims knowledge cannot be given to students but rather must be constructed by the learner through a combination of experiential learning and reflection. Experiences enable learners to develop schemata (constructs), mental models that can be modified and expanded through further experiences. Constructivism also emphasizes that the teacher is a facilitator of learning rather than a deliverer of content. Rather than feeding information, the facilitator helps learners come to their own understanding of the information, guiding them toward becoming effective thinkers. Time for reflection and discussion is of the utmost importance, as are the social aspects of learning and creating knowledge collaboratively with peers and educators.

CONSTRUCTIONISM

Inspired by constructivism and formally developed by Seymour Papert, constructionism agrees with the aforementioned concept of learning being actively acquired rather than transmitted. To this, Papert added that learning is most effective when the hands-on learning process results in a meaningful product, or "social object." Social objects are any creations—ranging from physical to virtual, concrete to abstract—that people attach meaning to and are able to talk about. In this view, learning is particularly powerful when students are engaged in constructing their own personally meaningful social objects to be shared as part of an inquiry process, serving as focal points for further experimentation, investigation, learning, and inquiry. Papert's book *Mindstorms: Children, Computers, and Powerful Ideas*, first published in 1980, remains a valuable resource for applications of constructionism through computational technologies.

DIFFERENCES BETWEEN CONSTRUCTIVISM AND CONSTRUCTIONISM

Many makerspaces combine concepts from these two theories. Sometimes it's difficult to discern the key differences. For further disambiguation between constructivism and constructionism, read the in-depth piece by MIT's Edith Ackermann. In a nutshell, she summarizes the difference as such:

> "Piaget's constructivism offers a window into what children are interested in, and able to achieve, at different stages of their development. The theory describes how children's ways of doing and thinking evolve over time and under which circumstance children are more likely to let go of— or hold onto—their currently held views. Piaget suggests that children have very good reasons not to abandon their worldviews just because someone else, be it an expert, tells them they're wrong. Papert's constructionism, in contrast, focuses more on the art of learning, or 'learning to learn',

Maker Ed

Student inquiry into
properties of water.
Photo: Opal School

and on the significance of making things in learning. Papert is interested in how learners engage in a conversation with [their own or other people's] artifacts, and how these conversations boost self-directed learning and ultimately facilitate the construction of new knowledge. He stresses the importance of tools, media, and context in human development."

Both theories share a child-centered view focused on empowering learners with active roles in constructing knowledge through powerful experiences. Both reject the view of children as mere receptacles of information and celebrate the capacity of children to make and share things of great value for each other and society.

REM Learning Center: Blended Approach Based on Constructionism

**Fab Lab Manager
Ryan Moreno**

Photo:
REM Learning Center

The most established learning approach we're influenced by is Papert's theory of constructionism. Our learning environment is designed to solicit playful exploration, encourage teamwork, and provide access to the use of tools and technologies that facilitate creative expression, empowering the child to extend the concepts being explored during creative play into a material form so that it can be shared with others and used to construct knowledge. Each child enters the school with unique perspectives and challenges. Our objective is to assist the child along their learning journey by providing a hands-on, creative, social, playful, and developmentally appropriate environment.

Outdoor play is essential for child development. In the same way, children need safe, creative learning environments with time and space for their imaginations to run and nontraditional equipment to construct knowledge, explore designed systems, facilitate a tinkering disposition, and provide a sense of maker empowerment.

We believe that lifelong learning happens whe you play, make, and share. We're investigating how the integration of methods—such as desi thinking, systems thinking, computational thin play, making, and tinkering—within both form and informal learning environments can be used to introduce 21st-century skills and insp a lifelong love of learning at an early age. We provide a safe environment where childre engage in a balance between creative play an guided play; are introduced to real tools that empower them to make and extend play; and have opportunities to share their creations and experiences, while receiving feedback from peers, family, and community.

Sample Project: Work with children ages fou to nine to design and make their own chairs for the studio. Look at the components that make up a chair, and using an open-source chair design as a foundation, children design a chair as a group, creating a tangible object that solves a problem (no chairs) and contribu to their community.

You may be asking yourself at this point: How do I decide which approach to take? If you ask any one of the spacemakers highlighted here, they would tell you that the answer certainly doesn't appear overnight. It takes time and experimentation to find the approach that works best for your staff, your youth, and the ultimate learning goals of your space. You may want to start with one approach first and dive deep o to let your inner chemist shine through by mixing and matching ideas from each un you arrive at your perfect blend. We encourage you to take the time to continually reflect upon the principles that guide the facilitation of learning experiences in your space and settle on an approach best suited to the needs of your community. There is no single maker education approach. What is *your* maker ed?

Putting It All Into Practice

Just as with the creation of your physical space, don't let the details stop you from diving in and getting started. Even without your learning approach fully developed, you can still put some important aspects of these ideas into practice and create meaningful learning experiences for your youth.

POINTS OF ENTRY

How to begin? You don't need to start from scratch or try something completely new. Many of the activities, lesson plans, or practices you already use can be easily modified by employing some of the ideas in this chapter. Try loosening up the structure, pulling back on prescriptive instructions, building in a little more time, and letting your young makers run with it!

If you're still searching for some accessible prompts to launch making experiences, here are a few ideas to get you started:

o **Free Play:** Invite and support imagination by providing materials and suggesting options. The main idea is to allow for creative, unstructured exploration. One option is to experiment with the construction sets outlined in Appendix C. Another is to provide old electronics, tools to take them apart with, and safety glasses, and invite children to disassemble the gadgets and put the components together in other interesting ways. (Look for safety tips in Appendix B.)

o **Skills:** Anchor an experience with the teaching and practice of specific skill sets. Alternately, start with the information or ideas you'd like to explore (whether STEM, art, social, etc.) and anchor discussion and projects within. For example, run a skill-building workshop to teach the group to solder, and then provide a simple electronics kit that involves basic soldering. Rather than presenting the initial idea, another option is to invite young learners to present something that they love to do—such as music, dance, debate, or a particular game—to their peers and help everyone develop this interest and the related skills. It's empowering to identify young learners who have specific skills and can take leadership roles in teaching and mentoring.

o **Personal:** Ask youth to think of a problem in their community that they would like to solve. Then, develop questions collaboratively to spark imagination, energy, deep interest, and connect to children's desires, interests, and goals. David Sengeh, president of Sierra Leone-based Global Minimum, notes:
> "In our woodworking workshop, a group of students chose to focus on the issue of waste management in their school. The school compound is usually littered with papers, bottles, and other garbage. Trash bins in public places and homes in Sierra Leone are also rare to find. Students therefore constructed a unique trash/recycle bin using only wood materials. They produced multiple designs and constructed a trash bin that can be easily replicated and emptied. The students hope to educate their school on waste management and are advocating for the adoption of their trash/recycle bin by many other schools and centers in Sierra Leone."

o **Competition or Exhibition:** Preparing for an event is a great way to anchor a project and set a deadline. Try tackling a project to present at a robotics competition, county fair, or local Maker Faire.

Maker Ed

A Maker Ed Young Makers participant and her cave exploration robot. Photo: Maker Ed

RE-EXAMINING ROLES

Evaluating the wide range of roles possible for educators, children, and their peers is important to creating meaningful making experiences. At Maker Ed, our philosophy is one of "Every Child a Maker." We believe that all children are born capable, creative, and deserving of opportunities to express themselves i multiple forms. The most powerful role adults can assume is that of facilitator and mentor, encouraging, guiding, sharing, but ultimately allowing children to develop processes and come to conclusions of their own accord.

The same tips that we offer to our Young Maker mentors can be helpful for other facilitators: "Mentors provide general support and motivation, facilitating teamwork and problem solving. Mentors sometimes act as sounding boards, fellow brainstormers, and timekeepers. Mentors do not have to have expertise in a specific area; rather, they help to outreach, network with others, and seek out answers."

One of the resounding benefits of maker education is the confidence that children gain from making. A great way to reinforce this is by empowering them to share their knowledge with their peers. At Toronto's MakerKids, one of their principles is "kids teaching kids." Facilitators identify areas where kids are experts, like in the building aspects of Minecraft, and have kids teaching classes. They also encourage children to share their knowledge online so others can benefit from their expertise.

Facilitators can promote student-centered learning by keeping an eye out for specific areas in which peers might support each other. For example, suppose you've helped a student learn to solder or witnessed a learner solve a problem. Ask, "How would you feel if I sent others to you when they need help with what you've just learned/accomplished?" In this way, you set up the student to share what they've learned, thereby recognizing and reinforcing the accomplishment while promoting peer-to-peer support.

THE POWER OF LANGUAGE

Language is perhaps the most important and powerful tool used within any makerspace. Words have the power to invite, inspire, and potentiate but also to shut down and exclude. We encourage you to deeply consider the language and overall tone used in your space. Part of the power of language is knowing when to use your voice at all. Exercising restraint at key times can invite new questions and ideas, empower youth, and help balance the voices in your space.

Powerful phrases like "I notice" and "I wonder" allow suggestions to be made without giving those suggestions the gravity and absoluteness that could shut down the creative process. They also convey attention and help show recognition in meaningful ways. Consider the difference between "That's awesome! Good job!" and "Wow, I see a huge amount of careful stitching! How did you develop the pattern to create such an intricate design? It looks super tricky. Could you show me more about how you did it? What would you think about helping others if they need it?" We believe language is so important that we've dedicated a page in Appendix D to offering ideas for helpful language to use.

Whatever language examples inspire you, think about the intention behind these suggestions rather than the exact words. Repetition of any phrase can diminish its power over time. Your observations and questions can be communicated in countless ways, such as beginning with "I see" or "It looks like" or "What about." You could simply state, "I'm curious about this. What would you like to tell me about it?" Children are masters at recognizing genuine interest and curiosity in all the ways you communicate, including your facial expressions and body language.

Nonverbal body language can be as powerful as the spoken word. Consider the difference between passing a child the next tool needed for a project versus allowing the child to decide which tool is needed. At times when you wish to exercise this restraint, it can be tough to override well-meaning adult reflexes to hand over what is needed right away. One approach is to strategically put your hands in your pockets or behind your back—keeping in mind that hands in pockets can be interpreted as signifying disinterest, so be sure you still show it other ways, such as leaning in. Another helpful gesture, rather than handing over a tool directly, is to place a useful tool or material nearby, allowing for discovery. This can be especially effective for subtly assisting someone who is struggling. Eye contact, even across a room, is also a powerful way to check in. Much can be communicated—such as reassurance—by a simple look, nod, and smile.

In conclusion, the environment, the materials in it, the approach, and the language and facilitation techniques used all contribute to creating a safe and creative space. Don't be afraid to experiment to find the approaches that work best for the purpose and values of your space and that serve your learning community optimally. The feedback will be transparent, and you'll know when you've created an environment where young makers can learn, grow, develop their own ideas, feel confident and empowered, and flourish. ═

SUSTAINABILITY

At this point, you've found a physical space, outfitted it with tools and materials, and explored the overarching approaches that will drive the space. Now, how do you staff your makerspace and keep it going? Collaboratively and by capturing and sharing the experiences—that's how!

We know how important a solid foundation and support system is to the success of a space. In this chapter, we explore the people and partnerships at the heart of your space, as well as the fundraising strategies, documentation, and evaluation that can help you gain more support from your stakeholders and the larger community.

Very Important People

As we saw in "Places to Make," a number of flourishing makerspaces were initiated by just one or two individuals passionate about spreading the joy of making. While one person may be the igniter, having a dedicated core team is important. Finding individuals who share in a combined vision for your space and bring a range of expertise within the team can be extremely powerful.

A prime, albeit aspirational, example is the Children's Museum of Pittsburgh's Makeshop. As Lisa Brahms notes: "With both practitioners and scholars in one department, there is constant exchange between the two: emerging theories are formed around observable interactions and, in turn, directly influence facilitation and design." Although you may not be starting out with this level of resource and expertise, putting together a small team with a range of skill sets is within reach.

MAKERS FROM THE COMMUNITY

Makers of various stripes are all around us, and many of them are willing to share their skills and knowledge. Where can you find them? A great resource for ideas is the last page of a booklet collaboratively created by Maker Ed and Girl Scouts USA, which lists a number of helpful suggestions. Here are a few:

o **Events** like Maker Faire, science fairs, and craft fairs
o **Clubs and community groups** based around interests like computers, model trains, and knitting
o **Friends and neighbors** with expertise to share from their careers or hobbies
o **Community organizations** like museums and libraries
o **Local professionals** such as carpenters, construction contractors, welders, electricians, plumbers, automotive mechanics, farmers, furniture makers, etc.

The key is to reach out and let folks know that you'd love to have them share what they know. Naturally, sharing via social networks can expand your reach exponentially, but posting paper flyers around your neighborhood also still works. When reaching out to community makers of all types, remember that the words "making" or "maker" might not be familiar. You might ask, "What do you love to do? Would you like to share and inspire others?"

Another way to find makers and also expand your offerings is to simply lend space for people to share their skills. At STEAMLabs, Andy Forest notes, "There are so many passionate artists, makers, and scientists in our city [Toronto]! After 6 p.m. every day is community time, available for community-run events." At OLÉ, they facilitate skill shares, where community members teach workshops based on what they already know, as well as repair cafes, where community members volunteer to help folks fix and modify their goods rather than having to purchase new ones. These models can add value without requiring a lot more resources.

MAKERS-IN-RESIDENCE

A number of makerspaces have had great experiences with maker-in-residence programs that help broaden their offerings of skills and bring community members to the space.

Brightworks school in San Francisco hosts one such maker-in-residence program, stating, "To further break down the walls that often separate school from the world, we invite artists, engineers, makers, writers, and craftspeople from all over the Bay Area to come into the school to use it like their own studio for a week." Students can watch the maker at work, and sometimes they're given the opportunity to collaborate or apprentice with the maker as well.

Teen Craft Jam.
Photo: Bubbler at Madison Public LIbrary

Others have experimented with specific artist-in-residence programs. One example is Madison Public Library's Bubbler. Trent Miller shares: "For the last year we've had a very successful artist-in-residence program. We invite a local artist to use the Bubbler space at the Central Madison Public Library as a studio for one to three months. The artist works in a space that is open to the public for questions and interactions, teaches classes in their work, and creates art in the space and the library. We've had a printmaker, a bookmaker, a woodworker, a performance artist."

The Free Library of Philadelphia also taps into the skills of artists in their community. As Sarah Winchowky notes: "All our mentors are also practicing artists of different kinds—we are writers, video makers, comedians, musicians, visual artists, and designers. We work to create a learning environment that fosters imagination and most all of our projects end up including some artistic elements, whether we're working with traditional art materials like paint, building squishy circuits, or doing chromatography experiments."

PARENTS, GUARDIANS, AND EXTENDED FAMILY

Utilizing the help of available parents and extended family has forever been a valuable resource in education. Not only are most parents and guardians deeply invested in seeing children grow and learn, inviting them to help gives them an opportunity to spend time making as a family, while sharing their own knowledge and skills. At the Children's Museum of Houston, Brent Richardson notes:

> "A primary tenet of the museum emphasizes the need to equip parents to serve as their children's most influential teachers. Therefore, the projects in which children are engaged do not separate them from their parents (or other adult caregivers) and provide parents with opportunities to coach and encourage, regardless of their own levels of educational achievement.

> "This approach helps to create a safe and supportive learning environment and also allows museum staff to serve the maximum number of families. In the museum's makerspaces, parents are either working on their own project next to their child(ren) or working on the project with their child(ren)."

Be sure to promote your programs and events with clear messaging about who is welcome to attend, and provide an inviting environment for family members by doing things like: offering a separate play area for children who may be too young to participate, providing bilingual facilitators if necessary, and finding a date/time that works for families (e.g., some parents work on Saturdays).

OTHER VOLUNTEERS

As we discussed earlier, children themselves are an invaluable source of knowledge, and many are happy to share what they know with the group. Makerspaces are also increasingly creating formal programs to train teens to become mentors for younger children. For example, Tehama County's Makerspace recently launched a capacity-building program for teens called Makerspace Ambassador. They have four local high school students who spend a few days a week in the makerspace working on their own passion projects, as well as aiding the makerspace staff. Ambassadors are selected based on recommendations, rather than grades, to help provide opportunities for those who might benefit most.

A lot of high schools have a service requirement, and volunteering at a makerspace is a neat way to fill it for the community at large. Similarly, summer programs employ youth counselors-in-training who may also be interested in volunteering.

In addition, many colleges and universities are filled with students looking for summer internships or projects to fulfill a course requirement. Most fraternities and sororities also have community service requirements. Having college students in your space can help provide important role models and near-peer mentors for youth.

Maker Ed

Maker Ed AmeriCorps
VISTA at Ravenswood City
School District.
Photo: Karl Mondon/
Bay Area News Group

National service programs may also serve a need in your community. A federal entity, the Corporation for National and Community Service runs several programs, including AmeriCorps and AmeriCorps VISTA, that may provide much-needed personnel for your space. Maker Ed is one of several nonprofits that are part of a STEM AmeriCorps initiative. Our Maker VISTA project focuses on eradicating poverty through maker education. Maker VISTA members work behind the scenes with community schools nationwide to help develop the systems and infrastructures to bolster the institution, allowing it to create more opportunities for the community to engage in making. These capacity-building services are the basis for ensuring that the work sustains and grows, impacting youth on a broader and deeper level.

Building a Culture of Support & Recognition

A vital part of sustaining any space is building a culture that recognizes and celebrates the roles of everyone in it. Through discussions, reflection, notebook use, and documentation, there are continual opportunities for youth and adults alike to develop habits of regularly noting and sharing attribution for ideas, inspiration, and support. Simple questions such as "Who helped me today? Who and what inspired me? Who did I help?" go a long way toward developing this culture. Giving credit where it is due and honoring contributions also helps with staff and volunteer retention. Every skill share, idea inspiration, assistance, or kind ear made visible adds to increased awareness of what each person has to offer the community.

A first grader shares her
gift to the school community.
Photo: Opal School

I offer the gift of kindness because when someone else feels sad or cries I can check in and see what happened. I can offer support by asking them, "Do you want to tell the person who made you feel bad how you are feeling?"

Putting peer-to-peer support front and center builds a safe community for idea-sharing, one where "Hey! Don't copy me!" becomes "I'm glad the wire whiskers on my mask helped give you the idea to use wire for hair on yours!" This has great potential social-emotional development benefits. Individuals who feel recognized are more likely to seek further ways in which they can share their gifts with the community. All spacemakers can model these behaviors and help establish routines and language to build a culture of contribution, attribution, and respect.

Partnerships

Partnerships with established organizations and institutions can provide a powerful support system. Some spaces are born out of partnerships and many spaces couldn't exist in the capacity they do without them.

As Andrew Coy of Digital Harbor Foundation notes:
"More important than anything else are effective partnerships with synergist outcomes. ... As an innovator, your job is to find the points of intersection that line up everyone's strengths, capacities, and self-interests appropriate If all of these things aren't in place, the partnerships will fall apart, often even before they get off the ground."

The saying "progress moves at the speed of trust" holds true when it comes to partnerships because they rely on interpersonal relationships. If you want to test the waters with an organization, try reaching out to them on social media, attending one of their events, or extending a personal invitation to one of your events. When you're ready to dive deeper and create a partnership that is truly mutually beneficial, it's important to set clear expectations about what each organization is bringing to the table, have a common understanding of the vision and purpose, and then set shared goals and objectives. Be honest about your organization's weaknesses and gaps but also about what unique strengths it offers.

The types of partnerships available are as varied as the kinds of makerspaces. This is an opportunity to be imaginative and look for unique ways to combine forces and make change. Here, representatives from three makerspaces share the types of partnerships that have benefitted them.

Millvale Community Library (MCL)
Brian Wolovich, President

"When the MCL was about to open, we connected with Lisa Brahms from the Children's Museum of Pittsburgh. They were implementing a project called the Mobile Makeshop, to take their well-known makerspace Makeshop on the road and seed other programs. They were looking for a library partner, and we were looking for programming opportunities. It was a match made in Pittsburgh.

"The programmatic components were developed under the watchful and thoughtful guidance of Children's Museum of Pittsburgh in the 2013–2014 school year. Since then, we've partnered with Maker Ed and our other partners to continue honing, building, and learning about how to best grow our efforts."

New York Hall of Science (NYSCI)
Janella Watson, Director of Early Childhood Education

"In 2010 we developed NYSCI Neighbors, a program designed to work with area schools and community-based organizations to directly engage our surrounding neighborhoods on how best to tailor our outreach efforts, exhibits, and programs to meet the needs of local families. A key part of this process included connecting with neighborhood teachers, principals, and parent coordinators, where we learned of an acute shortage of quality STEM education in the community's public schools, despite the vital importance of STEM learning in the 21st-century workplace."

STEAMLabs
Andy Forest, Chief Instigator

"The Centre for Social Innovation in Toronto and New York is a great partnership for us. The CSI is a social enterprise with a mission to catalyze social innovation. Our space is located in the CSI's 64,000-square-foot building in the heart of downtown Toronto. The hands-on making that STEAMLabs provides directly in their largest location is a big part of this. By partnering with them, we bring a purpose to our programs: making the world a better place.

"The Mozilla Hive Learning Network is also a fantastic group of organizations focused on digital literacy skills. We come together to share ideas and resources and to plan projects. Funding opportunities are frequently available, too."

Maker Ed

MAKING CONNECTIONS

When creating your space and thinking about sustainability, it's important to find a balance between being "heads down" in your work and being part of the larger movement in education. Conversations with the broader community can not only save you from reinventing the wheel but also form meaningful partnerships that could propel your organization forward. Here's a small sampli of opportunities that currently exist to connect with fellow maker educators.

The Association of Science-Technology Centers has a community of practice devoted to Making & Tinkering Spaces in Museums. The group has a lively listserv, as well as regular online meetings and discussion sessions. Social mec (Facebook groups, Twitter chats, etc.) has proven to be a very valuable way to stay engaged and form connections. The hastag #makered, started by K–12 teachers, has been highly active and has regularly scheduled chats online The Google group K–12 Fab Labs and Makerspaces consists of educators who share tips, tricks, and challenges about running and managing their spaces.

In addition to our online community, Maker Ed has offered several in-person events, supported local gatherings, and engaged sites in programs that help connect maker educators nationwide. Michelle Carlson from the Tehama Coun Department of Education reflects:

> "We have received great support from Maker Ed. The Making Possibilities Workshop was a huge source of initial inspiration. Also, the Bay Area The Bay Area Maker Educators group has been so helpful, nice, and inspirational. Being up here in Tehama County, these folks have given us a way to get out of our bubble and see what the rest of the world does with making. We are also a Maker Corps site this year."

Fundraising

Let's face it, when you hear the word sustainability, one of the first things that comes to mind is funding. Even if we'd rather it not be, money is a vital part of creating, maintaining, and sustaining a space. We know that without enough funds, it's incredibly difficult to bring your vision of a thriving space to fruition and keep it going. For those just getting started, this section provides resources, suggestions, and tips to help navigate the five main sources of funding for makerspaces: individual, corporate, foundation, earned income, and government grants.

INDIVIDUAL GIVING

For a space that directly serves the community, individual giving may be the best way to raise funds and can range from raising money from the families of the youth you serve to seeking people who are capable of making large contributions to your space. Remember, no matter what the scale, it's importa to build relationships that last: consider online newsletters, donor events, handwritten thank you cards from the youth who use your space, and other ways to keep your donors involved and invested in your work. It's important to be in touch with them multiple times throughout the year, not just when you're asking for money.

Although the timeline for you to receive funds can be relatively short (compared to how long a grant process can take), you shouldn't think of this as a "once and done" venture. The fundraising axiom that "people give to people, not causes" has been proven true time and again. Individuals will give more when they have a personal connection to the cause, and the more they feel connected and involved, the more likely they are to donate.

You might also want to have a focused fundraising campaign around the end of year or around a special event you're holding (refer to the Knight Foundation's Giving Day Playbook for inspiration). And although they will take a small fee, crowdfunding sites have also become a popular means to run this type of campaign. You can rally your friends, family, and maker community to spread your reach over a large group of people. Makers have had success with sites such as Kickstarter, Indiegogo, DonorsChoose, and Rally.

CORPORATIONS

If you're interested in reaching out to corporations, your board is a great place to start. Many have connections to local businesses, large corporations, or local branch offices of large corporations. Make sure to do your homework before attending a meeting with a potential funder and come prepared with multiple ways they might get involved beyond writing a check, such as in-kind donations (e.g., goods or equipment) or volunteer opportunities. Often, companies have employee-matching programs, where volunteer time leads to cash for your organization or where employee donations are matched by the company. Some corporations may also be willing to donate more substantial sums for naming rights to your space or a plaque or sign acknowledging their contribution.

Relationship building is always key—remember to thank the sponsor prominently on your website and/or in your space. You want to stay on the radar of these companies beyond their initial investment. If you build a good relationship, they may think of your organization first for future opportunities, when recommending volunteer opportunities to their employees, or if they have an end-of-year surplus in their budget.

FOUNDATIONS

Foundations are established expressly to support charitable activities, usually with money given from individuals, families, or corporations. Those that give grants look for organizations, projects, and programs that align with their own mission, so it's a good idea to talk with the program officer first to make sure your idea is a good fit before submitting a proposal or letter of interest. This is another wonderful opportunity to involve your board—and others in your community—by tapping into their networks. It can be easier to get the attention of a program officer if you're referred to them by someone they know.

When you're ready to have a conversation with a program officer, be prepared. You'll want to have several things at the ready: your "elevator pitch" (a short description of your work and its value concise enough to share in the time it takes for an elevator trip); your mission statement; and specific details about the work you're doing and the work you want to do, including data (how many people you serve, who they are, how you do it) and compelling personal stories. Although there may be a substantial amount of time between your initial conversation and when you receive any funds, the relationship you build can last for years. Remember that the first proposal may not be a fit, but it may start a conversation that could lead to something down the line.

EARNED INCOME

We can't forget to note that the work you do is worth money! Whether you know it now or not, many people will pay for it. Depending on who utilizes your space and what model makes the most sense for you, you might want to establish membership or drop-in fees, charge for classes on using equipment (such as 3D printers and laser cutters), or offer special workshops and classes for a fee. To still remain accessible for everyone, you can offer a sliding-scale model and/or scholarships. Sometimes asking people to pay even a small amount helps them put a greater value on your work. Be creative! A "Make Sale" is one unique way to earn income by selling the works created by the youth in your space. Companies may also be interested in hiring your youth to create signs or other collateral.

GOVERNMENT GRANTS

Grants.gov is a good place to start looking for government grant opportunitie Depending on the focus of your space, you might be a match for grants spanning from the National Science Foundation to the National Endowment for the Arts. Because these grants can be extensive and very time consuming to put together, it's best to talk to the program officer first about your idea. You may also consider finding a partner or a consultant that has received this type of grant in the past to help you navigate the waters. Additionally, look into state, county, and municipal governments in your area. Many have regiona opportunities that tie into their specific focuses and interests and may be a great fit for your space—especially if it connects to education or workforce development. Although time consuming, many government grants offer multi-year funding opportunities that can be extremely valuable to the sustainability of your space.

Remember that you're not alone. There are many resources available online an even in-person Meetup groups dedicated to fundraising support for nonprofits Organizations like Network for Good and the Foundation Center also offer lots of resources from fundraising plans to detailed information on funders to webinars on a variety of topics, many of which are free.

ocumentation

One of the most useful, powerful, and important actions to encourage in your makerspace is also oftentimes one of the most overlooked: documentation. Without it, what goes on in your space stays there, new audiences are harder to attract, lessons from experiences are not captured, and reflection is not as supported. Instead of being intimidated by it, think of it as merely capturing what is being done in whatever form is readily available to you. Ideally, this would be an integrated process where everyone documents: spacemakers, facilitators, and the youth alike.

What does documentation have to do with sustainability? Though it may not seem obvious, capturing the work of your makerspace is incredibly vital to sustaining the space and has many benefits:
o   Increases your organization's visibility
o   Shows recognition of efforts and ideas throughout the process
o   Provides active roles for youth
o   Provides new perspectives or responsibilities for educators
o   Contributes to institutional knowledge and culture
o   Gives back to the maker community by sharing experiences and examples
o   Provides concrete data for evaluation purposes
o   Captures programming and activities for marketing, funders, training, etc.
o   Offers a record of skills to show parents, teachers, administrators, college admissions, and job employers
o   Provides a meaningful context for reflection

How do encounters with materials lead to new discoveries?

Documentation also can play a huge role in supporting literacy development, artistic growth, skill building, and even safety. Imagine asking for written thoughts on what select tools and materials can do; their possible, best, and worst uses; and things to keep in mind regarding safety. Talking about these things together and capturing them can go a long way toward building skills and safe use of tools and materials. Over time, this documentation can provide an invaluable library of information and inspiration.

cumentation can be as
ple as a compelling question
d responsive images.
oto: Opal School

STORIES TO SHARE

One of the greatest gifts a makerspace can provide is sharing the thoughts and ideas of youth. What were the stories of their creations? What did they enjoy and learn? How and why? The stories of how anything is made, attempted, discovered, and explored are among the greatest things that will ever be made in a makerspace. They're especially powerful when captured by youth themselves. The kinds of opportunities that come from having well-documented and publicly available work cannot be overemphasized. Documentation can make a notable difference in attracting funding, support, and new audiences.

One tip to help your audience feel connected and invested in the stories you tell is to follow the old writing adage "Show, don't tell." Resist the urge to simply tell your audience about the experience, and instead, use sensory details that will help them conjure the experience in their own minds. Another way to get your audience involved is by helping them care about the people in it. Share details about your subjects and their unique personalities and perspectives to make them more relatable to your audience. Check out "Stories Worth Telling: A Guide to Strategic and Sustainable Nonprofit Storytelling" for further inspiration.

Perhaps the greatest benefit of sharing your documentation is expanding the influence of your space and giving back to the community. Blog, share all that you can on social media, and remember that you can keep it simple. In the world of social media, regular, short updates can have an equal or even larger impact than less frequent, larger posts. Even simple captioned images can be powerful and effective. Having a continuous presence, with variety of depth and complexity, is ideal.

Appendix E, as well as Maker Ed's "Sharing and Documentation" video, provide further suggestions on methods of documentation and ways of inspiring the practice.

Assessment, Evaluation, and Outcomes

As maker education gains traction and is widely integrated into classrooms and spaces, there remain good questions about its value, influence on learning outcomes, and impact on youth. For all stakeholders involved, it's fundamental to demonstrate how and why students engage with making and to capture their learning. Whether evaluating a specific maker education program or more generally seeking ways to assess learning through making, there's a rapidly growing base of research that makes the case for this work. Documentation of learning results in the qualitative and quantitative data needed to serve as compelling evidence to help you gain the support necessary to sustain your space.

Maker Ed's Open Portfolio Project (OPP) aims to develop a common set of practices for portfolio creation, reflection, sharing, assessment, and technology solutions to create an open, decentralized, and distributed lifetime portfolio system for makers. Focused primarily on student-centered documentation of work over time, the project makes the case for portfolios to serve as evidence of a student's learning and abilities, particularly the processes they encounter while making. Portfolios can be used by administrators, teachers, and others as an alternative means of assessment. As Maker Ed's Director of Programs Stephanie Chang notes, "Portfolios can showcase a youth's abilities, interests, thinking, and voice in a way that test scores and grades cannot." The Open Portfolio Project Research Brief Series shares practical findings, themes, and stories from its field research and survey.

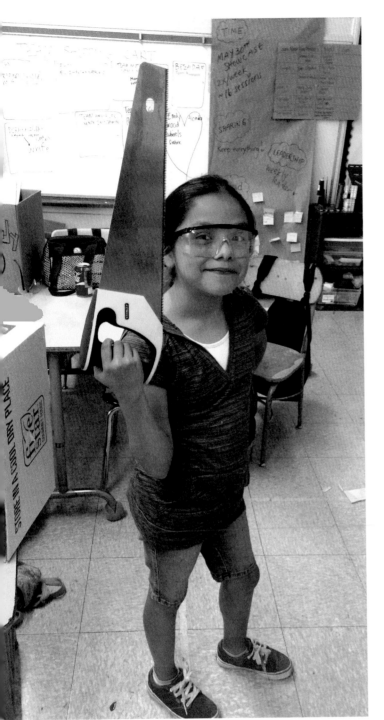

Photo: DIY Girls

Your desired learning outcomes will be unique and directly tied to the goals of your space. Documentation and evaluation will help make these goals and outcomes visible. Many existing toolkits and innovative research methods are available that may help you decide how and what you're most interested in tracking. Some spacemakers focus on subject content and others attempt to measure student engagement, interest, meaning-making, and the soft skills innate to learning and development. Here we list a sampling of them.

A team of researchers and practitioners, in collaboration with The Exploratorium, studied videos of learners engaging with tinkering activities. These video clips resulted in the Tinkering Library of Exemplars, which categorizes over 100 video clips to help articulate aspects of learning and facilitation. They welcome use and feedback from the larger field.

The Lawrence Hall of Science's Learning Activation Lab collects data around learning activities in science and art by focusing on the measurement of activation around a child's interest leading to persistent engagement. They've developed a set of instruments (e.g., surveys, interview, and observation protocols) that are free to experiment with in your space. In addition, their report on "Making the Future: Promising Evidence of Influence" contains a logic model intended to serve as an evaluation roadmap.

Agency by Design is a multiyear research initiative at Project Zero investigating the promises, practices, and pedagogies of maker-centered learning experiences. They have a white paper entitled "Maker-Centered Learning and the Development of Self" that introduces a definition of maker empowerment and a conceptual framework that guides the design (and evaluation/monitoring) of maker-based learning experiences.

"The Learning Practice of Making: An Evolving Framework for Design" by the Children's Museum of Pittsburgh is a report that applies a practice-based approach to learning and making in the context of a museum. The practices identified are observable and/or reportable evidence of learners' engagement in making as a learning process. The museum also hosts a website on Making & Learning that offers a variety of resources.

Maker Ed

To provide real-world context, let's take a look at examples of the systems three established makerspaces employ to assess the outcomes of their programs.

Free Library of Philadelphia
Sarah Winchowky, Project Coordinator

"We maintain daily sign-in logs at each site that list participants' names, ages, amount of time of participation, projects worked on, and any additional notes. This helps us keep track of returning participants, and participants' commitment to our spaces and programs is an important way in which we measure success.

"All mentors also compile monthly reports, which track progress made by various participants working on projects. Project completion and sharing is a way to measure success, but we believe that learning happens even if a project gets abandoned somewhere along the way. Another way we gauge success is by paying attention to whether participants feel ownership of the space and are working well with one another. When someone comes up to us and excitedly suggests an idea or a project, we know we've succeeded creating a space for exploration, creativity, and learning."

Children's Museum of Houston
Brent Richardson, Invention Convention Educator

"We have a commitment to outcomes-based evaluation, with the museum being the first in the nation to incorporate outcome logic modeling for program design and evaluation. Outcomes of engagement are evaluated annually, with instruments ranging from interviews with parents who use new exhibit components to third-party evaluations of efforts to increase learning at the museum and at home through the use of smartphones and tablets (see 21-tech.org for an example)."

Geekbus
Mark Barnett, Director of STEM Programs

"We track data about our students, such as age, socioeconomic level, and gender. We also measure interest, self-identification, and engagement using an instrument derived from a Society of Women Engineers study."

As we've seen in this chapter and throughout the playbook, the entire community can play roles in sustaining places to make. Staff, volunteers, families, and the young makers all play vital roles in creating supportive and inspiring environments, in building culture, and in forming connections and partnerships. Thriving spaces tend to have a diversity of partners, people, funding, and even documentation strategies—all working together to achieve their goals. Their strength is ultimately sourced from these differences and the variety of experiences and perspectives that they bring. =

CONCLUSION

We hope that, throughout this journey, you've been inspired by all the forms makerspaces can take and by the powerful roles they play for all in the community. As the stories have shown, the "stuff" is only a part of the story. So many have done so much with so little in the way of resources, thanks to the capabilities and endless potential of youth and the dedication of all supporting these spaces.

As you can probably imagine, we could have filled another hundred (and more) pages exploring the ideas we only touched upon here. Our goal, however, was to spark your imagination and guide you in a solid direction toward building and shaping a space that is grounded in the needs of your youth and community.

Our dream is that this playbook will continue to evolve and be shaped by your stories of the spaces it helps launch and nurture. We welcome your ideas, feedback, and discussion, and we hope you'll join our conversations via social media and online communities.

The work of makerspaces is glorious work. It can also be incredibly hard, and at times daunting, work. Always remember your initial motivations to create spaces to make. You care about providing children with positive, memorable, transformative experiences and believe in the power of making to inspire, educate, and empower youth. A positive impact on even a single child makes all efforts worthwhile. Expanding opportunities for all youth, especially those in the greatest of need, is valuable beyond measure.

On that note, we leave you with a story from Michelle Carlson of Tehama County Public School's Makerspace about the kind of impact that just one space can make.

"We had a boy here the other day who recently lost both of his parents very tragically. He's small, not athletic, quiet, struggling. He's a ninth grader. He got to explore code for the first time in his life and he loved it! When his guardian picked him up, she said he talked all the way home. He said that he enjoyed being able to explore and go at his own pace and wished all of school was like that. At the end of the conversation, he told her that he was going to go home and get on Code.org and that he thought he now knew what he would like to do with his life.

"In a moment, we can truly change lives. It's why we do this work so passionately."

Maker Ed

ACKNOWLEDGEMENTS

True to the spirit of makerspaces, this playbook was made possible through a joyfully collaborative process.

Without the energy, wisdom, and feedback of our National Working Group, who took time out of their busy schedules to share their expertise, this playbook wouldn't be what it is today. Our National Working Group members, in addition to a larger group of inspirational expert spacemakers, offered unique and robust windows into their makerspaces by completing our site survey. These survey results informed many of the examples used in this playbook, and we found them so helpful that we're sharing them in PDF format on our site. Many thanks to all members of our incredible brain trust!

NATIONAL WORKING GROUP

Sylvia Aguiñaga
Director of Curriculum
DIY Girls

Lisa Brahms
Director of Learning
and Research
Children's Museum of
Pittsburgh

Andy Forest
Chief Instigator
STEAMLabs

Susan Harris Mackay
Director of Museum
Center for Learning
Opal School Teacher
Researcher
Portland Children's Museum

Ryan Moreno
Administrator and
Fab Lab Manager
REM Learning Center
Play Make Share

Ira David Socol
Assistant Director for
Educational Technology
and Innovation
Ablemarle County
Public Schools

Janella Watson
Director of Early
Childhood Education
New York Hall of Science

SITE SURVEY BRAIN TRUST

Mark Barnett
Director of STEM Programs
Geekbus (SASTEMIC)

Michelle Carlson
Educational Technology
Director
Tehama County Department
of Education

Trent Miller
Library Program Coordinator
The Bubbler at Madison
Public Library

Brent Richardson
Invention Convention Educator
Children's Museum of Houston

Donna Sangwin
Founder and
Executive Director
ReCreate

David Sengeh
President of Board
and Cofounder
Global Minimum

Andrea Serrano
Deputy Director
OLÉ (Organizers in the
Land of Enchantment)

Aaron Vanderwerff
Creativity Lab Director
Lighthouse Community
Charter School

Sarah Winchowky
Project Coordinator
Maker Jawn at the
Free Library of Philadelphia

Brian Wolovich
President
Millvale Community Library

APPENDIX

MakerEd

MAKERSPACE PLANNING SHEET

	How do I imagine it being used? What do I hope to achieve?	What do I already have?	What do I still need? (Why do I need it?)	How do I get it? (From where or whom? When? At what cost?)
SPACE Think of the physical space as well as the atmosphere or environment you are trying to create.				
MATERIALS & TOOLS Consider whether or not each item will need to be maintained or replenished.				
PEOPLE Mentors, staff, volunteers, community partners, youth, etc.				

List some of the key takeaways from your interviews with youth.

Based on your youth's interest and the information in this table, brainstorm some project ideas for your space!

_____

_____

_____

APPENDIX B

TIPS FOR TAKING APART ELECTRONICS

Safe Practices for E-Waste Disassembly

Taking apart old electronics yields many treasures and discoveries, but it does present some dangers. Eye protection is always recommended. Often, while prying objects that are stuck, flying objects are a risk. There's an excellent summary of safety considerations for electronic devices on the iFixit site. Among the most important is making sure that anything being worked on is unplugged and is never plugged in after being taken apart. We recommend completely cutting off the power cords on devices such as old DVD players, clock radios, and VCRs. Most safety concerns can be addressed by being selective about what is provided to take apart.

DO NOT USE
- Laser printers (carcinogenic toner)
- Copy machines (toner)
- Microwaves (radioactive component)
- Cathode ray tube (CRT) TVs (deadly capacitor potential)
- Paper shredders (many sharp blades)
- Fluorescent tubes and compact fluorescent bulbs

OK TO USE
- Computers, laptops, hard drives, servers
- TVs and monitors: LCD, LED, plasma (no CRTs)
- Routers, hubs, modems
- Printers and scanners: inkjet, dot-matrix (no laser)
- Mobile phones, tablets, pagers, PDAs, GPS devices
- Telephones (rotary ones are gold mines!) and answering machines
- Keyboards, mice, microphones
- VCRs and DVD players
- Cassette players and stereo tape decks
- Webcams and digital cameras
- Battery-powered children's toys
- Scanners
- Loose components from any items above

Take-aparts that yield the greatest amount of potentially useful parts are those that include many moving elements. Older printers are especially great for this, as are VCRs, tape decks, and early CD and DVD players. Modern devices are still interesting and present a good challenge, as they're often very puzzle-like to take apart, with many hidden taps and use of glue in place of obvious large screws. Just be aware that these devices can also increasingly use security screws or none at all.

Maker Ed

Tools: Stars of the Take-Apart

Even without a full range of tools, many take-aparts are possible using only screwdrivers. Providing the correct sizes and types of drivers is important to making disassembly more effective, minimizing stripped screw heads, and reducing frustration. Most importantly, the right tool is the safest tool. A young maker struggling with the wrong-sized screwdriver, for example, is much more likely to slip or resort to potentially unsafe prying methods.

This list will help you get started with a wider range of tools for take-apart success:

- Screwdrivers, including a full range of Phillips and Torx ("star drive") sizes (Don't forget the tiny ones!)
- Security screwdriver bit sets, for screws especially common in modern, smaller electronics devices
- Magnetic parts bowls (These are fantastic to keep screws and small metal bits all in one place.)
- Wire cutters and wire strippers
- Nut drivers in SAE and metric sizes
- Clip leads and batteries, to test motors
- Hacksaw
- Needle-nose pliers
- Adjustable crescent wrenches
- Hammer, for when all else fails (Sometimes, you just have to smash something to get it apart!)
- Rotary cutter, such as a Dremel
- Small handheld vacuum (Older electronics often have a lot of accumulated dust in them.)

Have fun, and remember that when it comes to making things, you can always begin with un-making. Start by taking apart!

Photo: DIY Girls

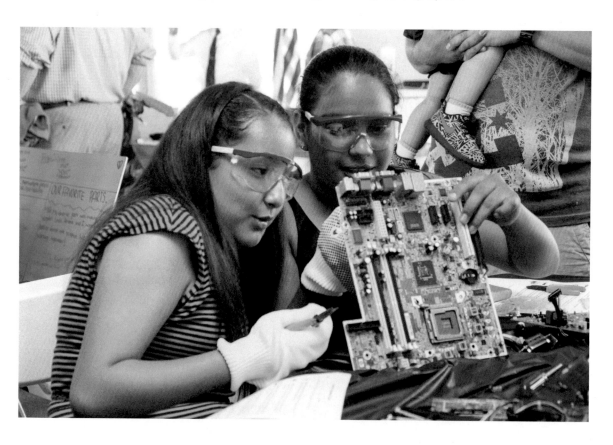

APPENDIX C:

CONSTRUCTION SETS
Planks, Bricks, Struts & Straws

Various systems of planks, bricks, struts, and straws are well worth including in any space as an entry point to building and reiterating structures. In the following table, we compare the affordances (described below) of four popular systems. We encourage you to create your own table and substitute the systems you currently use. Or simply use this tool to spark discussion about the affordances you notice and how each compares in the context of your space.

Mechanical Options How many mechanical elements, such as hinges, wheels, pivots, gears, and pulleys, are options built in within the system?

Fine Detail How small and complex are the details allowed by the system? Lego, with its many tiny, specialized pieces, allows for incredible fine detail. Plank systems have larger single elements that still allow complexity but not small-scale detail.

Electronics Options What are the depth of electronic options, such as motors, lights, remote control, or robotics, built into the system? All systems (except the planks) have various options that allow additional electronic complexity, though at relatively high cost.

Finding Factor How easy is it to find the piece(s) you're looking for? For example, Lego can be extremely detailed, but finding the right pieces can consume huge amounts of time. The plank systems, on the other end, only have a single element, so no time is needed to search.

Adaptability How easily can changes or additions be made to the system? Strawbees are the easiest, as straws can be easily cut to custom lengths. K'nex, because of its relatively strong and stable structures, has a different form of adaptability in that parts, such as batteries and motors, can easily be securely added with rubber bands, tape, or velcro straps.

Collaboration How easy is it to share building a single creation together? All work well in inviting combined modular structures (e.g., building a city together).

Element Durability How durable are the individual components of the system? How much repeated use will they sustain with reasonable amounts of care? Note that this does not necessarily have to do with the durability of the possible structures. K'nex elements are not as strong as Lego or planks, but their structures hold together better.

Construction Scale What are the ranges of structure sizes? Kapla and Keva can soar to surprising heights or span large distances with a sufficient number of planks. K'nex strut lengths can add up with minimal pieces, allowing the possibility of tall or long structures such as towers and bridges. Most Lego structures are smaller in scale.

Maker Ed

SYSTEMS	KAPLA/ KĒVA	LEGO	K'NEX	STRAWBEES
MECHANICAL OPTIONS				
FINE DETAIL				
ELECTRONICS OPTIONS				
FINDING FACTOR				
ADAPTABILITY				
COLLABORATION				
ELEMENT DURABILITY				
CONSTRUCTION SCALE	Medium to large	Small to medium	Small to very large	Small to large
NOTES	Pine versions are less expensive, while the maple Kēva option is much more durable. High-precision planks allow for complex creations and are easy to add to other wooden building blocks. Teacher discounts are available on request from Kēva.	Full systems range from super simple blocks (Duplo) to complex mechanics and robotics (Technic & Mindstorms). Expensive but very long-lasting. Standard 5mm LEDs are a close enough fit for the Lego hole size. Official motors are expensive but efficient and high quality.	Largest and strongest possible structures. Individual struts can be fragile. Motors and gears are options within the system.	Possibly the most economical, with the option to create your own connectors using various materials via a diecutting machine option. Electronics and microcontroller options. Standard 5mm LEDs are a perfect fit within many drinking straws. Connectors also act as cardboard rivets.

APPENDIX D

LANGUAGE USE

These examples are intended as springboards for experimenting with language use, in response to a variety of situations. A general rule of thumb is to search for language that discourages single-word responses (e.g., yes, no, OK, sure) and/or motivates action and engagement. We encourage you to use this as a point of personal reflection or as a spark for discussion among all those contributing to the space. What additional situations and possible language might you consider?

SITUATION	LANGUAGE IDEAS
A child is frustrated with their project or stuck with a particular challenge.	"It looks like you're really struggling with this. What kind of help do you need? I wonder if someone else has encountered the same problem. Let's check." "I hear your frustration. I would be frustrated too after so much work. Would you like to take a break and come back to it? Perhaps you can help others with the battery connection you got working earlier?" "That doesn't make any sense to me either. How cool is it that we have this mystery? I wonder what's going on? When you figure it out, can you tell me so that I can share it with everyone? If not, we can all work together to figure it out."
You'd like to invite conversation and learn more about a project.	"Whoa, that's a crazy number of LEDs and wires! I see some LEDs are on, while others turn off when you plug that one in. What are your ideas about what's happening? This would be handy as an example of how complicated this all can be. How would you feel if I shared it?" "That's an awesome and surprising use of felt, leaves, and wire. What's the story about how and why you chose these materials?"
You want to reinforce engagement, persistence, and a community of shared support.	"Wow, you really stuck with this and worked through all of those problems. Would it be OK if I sent others to you for help with this kind of thing?" "Have you drawn any of these setups? I'd love to be able to share them with everyone." "Can I take a picture of this to use as an example if someone gets stuck? What else do you think might be helpful to share?" "I notice you've worked incredibly hard on this and have still taken time to help others when they've been stuck. I wonder about where you got your inspirations and who might have helped you. Did any ideas come to you when you were helping with other projects?"
A young maker is having a hard time getting started with open-ended explorations.	"I hear that you're having a hard time getting started and would prefer an example. I do have some if you'd like, but how about waiting a bit and seeing what others are trying out? Perhaps something will inspire you. Try just messing around first, just playing and having fun. I'll check back with you in a bit to see how you're feeling." "I do have something that I'd like to show later as a possibility. Can I show it to you first and see what you make of it? I could use your help figuring out what kinds of things it might be useful for. I'd love to have you share it and your ideas, if you like."

Maker Ed

METHODS OF DOCUMENTATION

Photo: Maker Ed

There are many ways to capture and share children's thinking, work, play, and projects. In this appendix, we provide brief tips and suggestions for methods of documentation using notebooks, photo, video, and audio. Each approach can be used by anyone in your space. Youth, in particular, always provide unique perspectives given the tools to document their own efforts and those of their peers. You'll be especially amazed by the perspectives offered by the youngest of makers.

Notebooks

Comparing invention notebooks hacked with electronics.
Photo: Opal School

Before looking at modes of documenting involving gadgets, let's pay homage to the simplest, most accessible tools to start with: a notebook and pen. The humble notebook can become a powerful record of ideas, prototypes, processes, and mistakes, providing a focal point for reflection and iteration.

However notebooks are used, regular use can encourage growth in writing, drawing, dreaming, planning, and sharing. Any notebook will do. They can even be made more personal and fun by encouraging modifications and customization.

Simply asking, "Can I take a look at your notebook? I'd love to see your ideas!" can be incredibly empowering and encouraging of regular notebook use. Entries can also become a source of project ideas, intriguing and meaningful questions, and thoughts that spark excitement among peers when shared and recognized.

Photo and Video

A note of encouragement from 10 y.o. Maxx.
Photo: Maker Ed

We live in an era where quality cameras are now ubiquitous, especially in the form of most smartphones. How might we make best use of them for documentation purposes? How might we also empower youth in our spaces to capture and share their work, play, and perspectives?

It's powerful to hand a camera to a student and ask for their eye on things. This can also provide a positive role for anyone seeking to take a break and offer ways for youth to see, share, and show appreciation for all that goes on in the space. Youth see things and take images in a way that vastly differs from adults. You'll appreciate their unique vision.

For spacemakers, cameras can play pivotal roles in both restraint and engagement when it comes to supporting youth-centered approaches. Taking on the role of documenter allows educators to actively roam and see what's happening without necessarily directing. It provides a way to focus attention toward what is being made while showing care and curiosity.

Often, the majority of photos taken of project work are those of a child posing, looking directly at the camera while holding up their final creation. While these kinds of photos can be effective in showing appreciation for and value of the product, candid shots throughout the entire process show a fuller story and can capture genuine moments of triumph, collaboration, struggle, and joy.

Still, care must be taken to respect the space of youth at work and play. Often, it's enough to ask permission to record their work and to assure them that you understand if they would prefer some privacy.

This also touches on a larger issue: since we're mainly focusing on youth makerspaces in this playbook, it's important to be mindful of how images and videos featuring children are used. Establishing rules and managing expectations in your space is essential. Getting signed photo releases from parents or guardians is one way to ensure consent of use. Some folks avoid using a child's full name in any public-facing content for safety reason, while others deem this unnecessary. There's a wide range of rules. Tailor yours to suit the needs and desires of your community.

PHOTO AND VIDEO SHOT LIST

Here are some ideas to help encourage a variety of truly useful and versatile moving and still images.

o   Setups: Materials and environment "before" shots, including the space and tables
o   Wide-angle context shots: Where is this happening? What does the whole environment look like?
o   Medium and small-group shots
o   Close-ups of hands working with tools and materials, as well as of faces showing emotion
o   Table-level shots showing work and faces in the same shot
o   Overhead shots
o   Documentation of other forms of documentation (How very meta!)
o   Before and after pictures of the space: Helpful for maintaining organization by providing an image of how the space should ideally be left after an activity while celebrating the creative chaos of making

Yes, this can result in a large amount of media, perhaps too much. Keep in mind that photos and videos are only useful when you can locate them. It helps to select, curate, organize, and label/tag photos soon after taking them. Having youth, volunteers, and family members lend a hand can make the task more manageable.

Maker Ed

Sounds of Making

There's great value in capturing just words and sounds. Removed from images, issues like permissions and technical considerations like lighting are removed. The same phones and tablets we use as cameras are also audio recorders. Some applications even continuously record audio in a buffer and only save a selected period of time when you push a button, for example, after an amazing reaction, ideation, or celebration.

Recording discussions can lead to amazing content. Transcribing conversation can take it to another level, providing quotes and showing the evolution of ideas and collaboration. This is yet another role that can be taken on by a volunteer.

A last note about sound: It's actually among the most important, yet often neglected, aspects of video. Poor sound can take away a huge amount of the impact of even the most beautiful moving images. If you have the means and choice, investing in decent microphones can pay off tremendously. Still, even poor-quality audio can be transcribed, making the voices of youth more visible

It's also important to take breaks from documentation. The "fear of missing out" on the perfect shot can, at times, interfere with other aspects of the moment, including simply experiencing and enjoying it. As much as we encourage documentation, fantastic work still happens, even if it's not recorded in some way other than memory and the personal impact of the experience. ☰

Photo: CoLab Tinkering

Made in the USA
Middletown, DE
18 August 2018